C000130844

HAUNTED
SUFFOLK

Withdrawn
from
Suffolk Libraries
30127 06903537 1

HAUNTED
SUFFOLK

PETE JENNINGS

TEMPUS

Dedicated to my dear friend and colleague from Original Gemini Ghost Tours, Ed Nicholls.

Frontispiece: A Suffolk Harvest. During the Suffolk traditional summer harvest, lunch – often bread, cheese and cold tea – may have been brought to the field for the workers, by their family. Some farmers provided beer for them also at this time, or even a harvest 'horkey' supper with home-spun entertainment. Lots were drawn to see who cut the last sheaf (containing the corn spirit) and corn dollies were made from it. Strangers entering the field while the harvest was in progress would be expected to treat the harvesters after they 'hollered largesse' – a traditional shouted greeting and challenge.

First published 2006

Tempus Publishing Limited
The Mill, Brimscombe Port,
Stroud, Gloucestershire, GL5 2QG
www.tempus-publishing.com

© Pete Jennings, 2006

The right of Pete Jennings to be identified as the author of this work has been asserted in accordance with the Copyrights, Designs and Patents Act 1988.

All rights reserved. No part of this book may be reprinted or reproduced or utilised in any form or by any electronic, mechanical or other means, now known or hereafter invented, including photocopying and recording, or in any information storage or retrieval system, without the permission in writing from the Publishers.

British Library Cataloguing in Publication Data.
A catalogue record for this book is available from the British Library.

ISBN 0 7524 3844 1

Typesetting and origination by Tempus Publishing Limited.
Printed in Great Britain.

SUFFOLK COUNTY COUNCIL		
	06903537	
Bertrams		13.07.06
133.1094		£8.99
781785		

Withdrawn from Suffolk libraries'

CONTENTS

ACKNOWLEDGEMENTS

My grateful thanks to the various organisations and individuals that have permitted me to quote from their experiences and writings, including in no particular order: Suffolk County Archive Offices in Bury St Edmunds and Ipswich, Ivor Bunn, Suffolk & Norfolk Paranormal Investigations, Betty Puttick, BBC Radio Suffolk, The Ghost Club, Tony Ellis, Ghosts UK, Paranormal Dimensions, *East Anglian Daily Times*, British Paranormal Alliance, ParanormalDatabase.com and Graham Tilt.

Other publications by Pete Jennings
The Gothi & the Rune Stave (Gruff, 2005)
Pagan Humour (Gruff, 2005)
Suffolk Ghosts *Video* with Richard Felix (Past in Pictures, 2004)
Spooky Suffolk *CD*, with Ed Nichols (Gruff, 2003)
Old Glory & the Cutty Wren *Book & CD* (Gruff, 2003)
Mysterious Ipswich (Gruff, 2003)
The Northern Tradition (Capall Bann, 2003)
Pagan Paths (Rider, 2002)
Supernatural Ipswich (Gruff, 1997)
Northern Tradition Information Pack. (Pagan Federation, 1996)
Pathworking (Capall Bann, 1993)
Gippeswic Magazine – Editor (1992–1995)
No Kidding *CD* – Pyramid of Goats (Gruff, 1990)
Chocks Away *Cassette* – WYSIWYG (Athos, 1988)
Awake! *Cassette* – WYSIWYG (Homebrew, 1987)
The Wild Hunt *DVD*. Produced by Will Wright (Film Tribe, release due in 2006)

You can also visit Pete Jennings' homepages at www.gippeswic.demon.co.uk

INTRODUCTION

It may seem surprising to declare in the first line of a book like this that I don't believe every supernatural story I hear. I do actually think that tricks of the light, the effects of alcohol and drugs, genuine mistakes, as well as wild exaggeration and tall tale-telling, play a part in diminishing the power and depth of people's more genuine occult experiences. One may dismiss maybe ninety-five per cent of the stories told by explaining them away in various fashions, yet there still remains an unexplained kernel of these for which no explanation is yet convincing. It is those stories I like to concentrate on.

I have come to believe that most people have some sort of psychic ability to a greater or lesser extent, whether it be seeing, hearing or simply sensing 'things not of this world'. Unfortunately, many suppress it, either because they are frightened or don't want to be ridiculed. How many children have had their natural ability thwarted by adults dismissing their 'imaginary friends?'

How many adults have been convinced that anything occult must be 'the work of the devil' despite their own religion's belief in an afterlife? Animals are not subject to that same oppression, so are often a very good guide to something supernatural and will frequently react by snarling a defense or avoiding the source.

As you will find out later in the book (*see* 'A Family Story') my mother first introduced me to ghosts when I was thirteen. Her tale lead me to enquire about other supernatural stories and I have collected them for forty years since then, as well as ending up spending the last decade running Original Gemini Ghost Tours in Ipswich with my friend Ed Nichols. Indeed, I am very grateful to him and the many people who have approached me on the tour and freely told their own tales to add to my repertoire. It is a great way for me to show off my home-town, combining a novel approach to its history with the supernatural.

After forty years of searching, with the occasional odd feeling but nothing more concrete, I have finally experienced a ghost at the house of my next-door neighbour. After all those years of cold, damp midnight vigils I saw a ghostly lady at 3 o'clock on a sunny afternoon. Clearly, old buildings do not have the monopoly on ghosts – our semi-detached pair was built on an orchard in 1971. I have never personally gone out with measuring devices, but think that there is value in the scientific approach. It is a pity that so many investigative societies end up splitting between the scientists and those who prefer the more intuitive, experiential approach. Ideally, co-operation would achieve a more rounded picture of what is going on.

I never think it is my job to convince people of the existence of ghosts or other supernatural phenomena. I believe most people are perfectly capable of making up their own minds having been told the tales. Funnily enough, some of the people who accompany me on ghost tours profess to disbelieve such tales, but still find them interesting, particularly in illuminating the often unwritten history of our delightful corner of England. Others believe on the basis that 'there's got to be something else out there'.

Who knows what a ghost is? Only the dead are experts on that and they rarely communicate. There are theories about certain characters being drawn back to a particular place, or with unfinished business to fulfil. Others talk of walls being like video recorders, replaying vivid events of the past. Whatever the explanation, there is a surprisingly large percentage of the general public who believe that there is 'something to it'. Some of my informants have been doctors, policemen and others; their reputations would be harmed if I exposed their identities, but yet they still feel impelled to tell their tales to me. I try to emphasise that not all ghosts are ancient and that we seem to generate new ones occasionally while others fade away. It would certainly be overcrowded if everyone became a ghost and hung around forever.

Despite the huge flat fields of wheat, sugar beet and potatoes, the rural landscape of Suffolk has many contrasting areas and I have tried to divide it within the book as the West, Central and East. The West includes the mysterious fens, with their flint-fronted cottages, Newmarket Racecourse and historic Bury St Edmunds. The Central part is dominated by the county town of Ipswich and port of Felixstowe. The East includes our gloriously picturesque East Coast with England's most easterly point at the seaside resort of Lowestoft and other beautiful spots such as Southwold, Woodbridge and Framlingham and delightful market towns such as Beccles, Bungay, Halesworth and Saxmundham.

The area has a rich history and more ancient treasure has been recovered here than almost anywhere else in the UK, from the internationally important Sutton Hoo Saxon ship burial, Hoxne hoard and Mildenhall Roman treasure to assorted gold torcs and caches of coins. Yet many would consider the timbered cottages of its wool towns and collection of churches and castles to be the real treasure of what was once known as 'Silly Suffolk'. The term derives from the Anglo Saxon *Selig South folk,* referring to the county's holy status, due to important shrines at Bury St Edmund's, Woolpit and the Madonna of Ipswich, the many monastic houses and the route on to Walsingham in Norfolk. I am unashamedly patriotic about my home county and have ancestors reaching back at least to the late 1600s buried in it.

Although mainly unrecognised by its own inhabitants, Suffolk has splendid continuing folk traditions of music, dance and song, the envy of most other areas of England. Because of its rural nature and late flowering of professional entertainment, the Saturday night sing-song, step dance or tune in the pub survived for longer here, so singers of my generation had the benefit of a living oral tradition to draw upon, while others had to rely on written and recorded sources.

Suffolk has spawned a hardy race, bitten by the east wind and invaded by many cultures. There is even a strong belief in many that we have been more recently invaded by the famous Rendlesham Forest UFO near USAF Bentwaters American airbase.

The Roman invaders felt the fury of the Briton, Boudicca and her Iceni tribesmen. Later the conquerors built a chain of coastal fort defenses against Saxon pirates at places such as Walton by Felixstowe and Burgh near Beccles, but the pirates became settlers in their turn before facing the Vikings (some of whom eventually also settled) and the Norsemen who came via France; the Normans. The Normans were harried by Hereward the Wake and his loyal Saxons.

Outsiders frequently confuse the slow, broad dialect with Norfolk, yet there are subtle differences that separate the two and specific dialect words such as *barnabee* for a ladybird and *dwile* for a dishcloth. The visitor is unlikely to get some local person elaborating a fancy tale for their delight. Outsiders are naturally viewed with a suspicion, probably dating back to feudalism and the taciturn, quiet, unexcitable way of the Suffolk person is the expected social norm. It is partly because of that I have written this book, in the hope that these tales will not be lost to a newer generation of residents or visitors to this wonderful county.

I would, however, advise you to be careful in seeking out the locations of the many psychic phenomena you will read about. You never know when you may discover another!

Pete Jennings
January 2006

ONE

WEST SUFFOLK

The Fate of Fred Archer

In his day, Fred Archer was a most successful and well-loved jockey, frequently appearing at Newmarket's famous racecourse, which has races recorded back as long ago as 1619. He won the Derby five times and over a dozen other classic races. The death of his wife after only one year of marriage sent him to drink though and he died in 1886 at the age of twenty-nine. Since then his ghost has often been reported and horses have frequently shied or swerved at a particular spot near Newmarket. Both jockeys and the general public have reported seeing him, still riding a fast galloping horse.

A Kentford Grave

There is a connection between a special grave here and the preceding story; on the verge of the B1506 one can see an isolated grave marked frequently with flowers. A young gypsy boy had a job shepherding some sheep. When one went missing he was sure that the suspicion with which he and his race were viewed would result in him being blamed. Rather than face the shame he took his own life and was buried close to the tree upon which he hanged himself, not being allowed to be interred in consecrated land due to his suicide. Some superstitious race-goers check out the colours of the flowers on his grave just before Derby day, since they are said to predict the colour silks of the winning jockey.

Magic and Mystery

About a decade ago Anglia TV's *Magic & Mystery Show* was at the Elizabethan Kentwell Hall, Long Melford. The house had a number of ghosts, one of which used to sit on the bed of a daughter of the household. Maybe it is the ghost of a lady of Kentwell who had a ballad written about her 200 years ago, or the body from the walled garden. Other spectres include a kitchen girl looking out of the window, a coach and horses and Young Aimee.

The Hall also shares a claim, along with other locations, to a story that became the basis of a popular Victorian ballad, 'Oh the Mistletoe Bough'. In it, the daughter of the house marries her sweetheart, Lovell, just before Christmas. Suggesting a game of hide and seek, to entertain the guests, she leaves them to hide herself. Before she does, she tells her new husband to be sure to find her first and she will reward him with a kiss. Lovell and the guests hunt high and low, but cannot locate her. In the end they can only conclude she has run away and had used this as a ruse. The song lyrics were written by T.H. Bayly (1797–1839) but are believed to be based on an older legend. Many years later, an old chest is opened in a long forgotten corner of the Hall. It contains the skeletal form of the bride, with her bridal wreath around her head. The chest must have clicked shut during the game and became her living tomb.

The nearby Bull Hotel, built in 1450, also has its own story. The Anglia TV team also stayed overnight there; all, that is, except one cameraman who gave up the chance of an excellent meal on the basis he had experienced a disturbing night there in the past with another crew. He would not elaborate, but the story of Richard Evered, who was murdered in the hallway there in 1648, may give a reason for the cameraman's reluctance. Roger Greene was quickly identified as

Above: *The stallion statue of Newmarket, a town dominated by horse racing, breeding and sales.*

Right: *The Gypsy Grave, on the B1506, Kentford, where a boy who committed suicide is buried.*

Above: *Kentwell Hall, Long Melford, the home of many ghosts.*

Left: *The Bull Hotel, Long Melford, scene of a murder and a disappearing corpse.*

Evered's murderer, tried and executed. What makes the case strange though was what happened to the victim. The body was left in a side room overnight, but disappeared and was never seen again, so his relatives who came to the inn the next day had no body to bury.

His ghost still haunts the Bull Hotel and there are frequent sudden drops of temperature at several spots there, as well as poltergeist activity of moving objects, footsteps and crashing noises. A couple staying in room 4 heard a crash of china outside. Instead of a dropped tray and an embarrassed maid outside, they found no one else about, in fact, there was nothing or nobody around at all.

The Dauntless Girl

Long Melford (literally the 'long mill ford') has another rather macabre tale to tell. Four farmers shared drinking sessions at a farmhouse. Mostly their conversation centred on agriculture, until one night when the ale ran out. Walter Scase, the host, being a little embarrassed, thought that he could send his housekeeper Rebecca to the Greyhound pub to fetch another jugfull. The others thought that she might be frightened to go out alone at this late hour, particularly as the route crossed the churchyard, but her master said she was a plucky girl and took a wager from Henry Sale that she would not complain. He was right and Henry paid up while she fetched more beer from the Greyhound pub down the lane.

The four met again another week and Henry had a plan to recoup his loss. He bet the others (including John Postle and William Moss) that she wouldn't go into the church crypt and fetch a skull. The others accepted and Rebecca was summoned. She looked a bit askance at their request, but went off straightaway without comment. On reaching the crypt she cautiously entered and made for the nearest skull.

'Not that one – my father!' boomed out a voice. Starting, she reached for its neighbour. 'No, not my mother!' the voice continued. Rebecca searched around and spotted two more skulls. 'Do not take my brother!' the doom-laden voice intoned. Without waiting for any more warnings, Rebecca grabbed the remaining skull and scuttled for the door, while ghastly cries pursued her.

She did not stop until she reached the farmhouse, where breathlessly she retold her tale. The four were dumbfounded and frightened, but believed they ought to investigate. They found the body of the verger, bribed by Henry to thwart her efforts, dead by the crypt door, a sheet still partly wrapped around him. It was reckoned he had suffered a heart attack with the excitement of the trick.

Rebecca didn't think much of the mean trick that had been played upon her and went to work for the local squire. He had a trouble getting staff because of his mother's ghost haunting the place, but Rebecca rose to the challenge. One day, she encountered the ghost in the cellar, who told her to lift a stone and find two bags of gold. She could keep the smallest, but the second was the squire's inheritance and should be given to him. Now that the ghost had got her message across, she need tarry there no longer. It was true what the spirit had said, but resourceful Rebecca thought that the squire had enough wealth already, so told him that the large bag was hers. Lusting after both her and the rest of the gold, he proposed marriage, but he turned out to be a cruel and drunken husband, so perhaps she suffered for her deceit.

The Lament of Lavenham

The pretty wool town of Lavenham, with its timbered buildings and spectacular church, has one lamentable tale to tell. A lady working at the Swan Hotel was desperately disappointed in being passed over for promotion. She ended up hanging herself and regularly haunts one of the upper rooms.

Lurking in Lidgate

It is believed that John Lydgate (1375–1461) took his name from the village of Lidgate. He was a poet and translator of books at the Benedictine Monastery in Bury St Edmunds. He inherited a house in Lidgate, which he gave to monks as a travelers' hostel. They often commented on the smell of delicious cooking despite none being done at the time. In the early 1940s a man walking home one night saw a figure of a monk walking about a foot above the ground, with just a void where the face should be.

An 'Appening at Ampton

Back in the 1940s, when Suffolk was the home to many of the wartime airfields, a young boy walked down towards Callow Hill Lane, Ampton. The wartime propaganda said to look out for strangers, since they might be German spies and saboteurs. He certainly had not seen the man

The Lavenham Swan, where a lack of promotion meant tragedy.

and his dog in the neighbourhood before, where almost everyone knew everybody else. Spy he might not have been, but spook he was. The man and dog just disappeared as they reached Callow Hill Lane.

The Killingback Killer

In 1690 at the Place Farm in Haverhill, an infamous murder occurred. Dilly was a young boy, in the care of the parish, who had been given lodging at the farm in exchange for work. Farmer Killingback beat him to death. The boy's ghost was said to haunt the area for fifty years, before finally being exorcised by a minister.

A Traitor's Reward

> To Ulfkel's land came Olaf bold,
> A seventh sword-thing he would hold.
> The race of Ella filled the plain –
> Few of them slept at home again!
> Hringmara Heath was a sword bed of death:
> Harfanger's heir dealt slaughter there.
>
> And Otlar sings of this battle thus:-
> 'From Hringmara field the chime of war
> Sword striking shield, rings from afar.
> The living fly; The dead piled high
> The moor enrich; Red runs the ditch.
>
> The country far around was then brought in subjection to King Ethelred, but the Thingmen and the Danes held many castles, besides a great part of the country.

From the *Saga of Olaf Haraldson in Heimskringla*

The Danish occupation of Thetford, over the Norfolk border and two associated battles are very interesting from a psychic phenomena point of view. One battle was at Ringsmere, then known as Hringmara Heath in Ulfkel's land, which was held by Ulfkel Snilling, on the 5 May 1010 to the north on Wretham Heath. The Norseman Ulfcytel fought it at Easter and several important Saxons were slain, including: the King's relative Athelstan; Oswy his son; Wulfric son of Leofwin; and Edwy brother of Efy, as well as many others. It was said that Thyrkel Myrehead first began the flight of Saxons and the Danes plundered and burnt for three months.

The other battle was 140 years earlier, to the south in Suffolk, probably at Rhymer Point, which also has mere or natural lake. It was fought in 870, between Barnham to the South and Thetford to the north. The Viking Ingvar had previously martyred King Edmund.

At Tutt Hill, Barnham (or alternatively Howe Hill, the site of a burial mound) a Saxon traitor, Tutt, advised the Vikings how to gain access to the town, which was defended by two forts, a river and earthworks. He hoped to be richly rewarded by the invaders when they had gained their booty, but honour and faithfulness were as important virtues to them as to their Saxon opponents, so his reward was a noose hung from a tree here. He is alleged to still occasionally appear there, clutching his throat.

The Creatures of Great Barton Mere

No warlike stories are attached to the watery mere at Great Barton, near Bury St Edmunds, but two nearby houses have their own mysterious tales to tell.

The owners of one property regularly let a pair of pet zebra finches out of their cage to exercise, as long as the door to the room was firmly closed. Imagine their horror on returning to find them both dead with blood around their beaks. The room had remained closed for two hours and the owners' dog (who refused to enter the kitchen) could not have entered. The house also has a 'grey lady' ghost, who walks through the lounge and up the stairs.

An animal also features in the story of another house in the area. An elderly lady reported that the head of a small dog, something like a Jack Russell, would follow her about. Characteristically, the head tilted slightly to listen to her talking, despite having no body attached or a tail to wag!

Giant Footsteps

There is a corny old joke about a policeman being asked, 'What steps would you take if you encountered something frightening?' He replies, 'Blooming great big ones!' Maybe his advice would ring true to the late-night traveller near Aspal Hall on the road from Beck Row, near Mildenhall to Holywell Row. He heard giant, heavy footsteps coming up from behind him. Turning to see who was making them, he was blasted by an icy draft, as an invisible 'something' rushed past him. More frightening than that was the fearful voice that cried, 'Don't fear me, fear my follower!' Needless to say, the traveller made some pretty rapid footsteps of his own after that.

The Green Mist

Beck Row and Mildenhall (from the Old English for 'place at the middle nook') form a gateway to the East Anglian Fens; those once flooded watery hinterlands that occupy an area running from Suffolk into Cambridgeshire and Norfolk. Dutch engineers once drained many of them by channeling their waters into vast long dykes and drains. This opened up the area for large-scale agriculture on the rich black silt, as opposed to some of the more traditional trades such as eel fishing and wildfowling that supported the isolated and fiercely independent Fen Tiger communities. It is difficult to appreciate how different the landscape is today from the eleventh century when the great English guerrilla-fighting hero Hereward the Wake defied the Norman invaders from the Isle of Ely, which was surrounded with water for two miles.

Such an area of mist-shrouded reed beds and sullen grey skies still give a feeling of menace sometimes today. It must have seemed like that when a young girl complained of the dreary wretchedness of their isolated existence in the midst of winter, when all was grey, cold and lifeless, only to be scolded by her mother who told of what happens to those who wish for the green mist out of season: they slowly decline and perish when the first flowers are picked in their presence. But it was too late. The curling vaporous tendrils of marsh gas and ague-inducing damp worked upon the sweet young body of the once lively maiden. She was confined to bed, tormented by the calls of the booming bitterns and harsh heron cries.

When spring finally came, the girl was weak, but more cheerful and was eventually able to rise from her bed and look out of her window. One day a brisk young lad walked by and called hello. She came to look forward to his passing each morning and evening on his way to cut reeds. When he shyly asked if she would like to go for a walk with him one evening after work, the colour came back to her cheeks and her mother was pleased to see her tidy her appearance and eat a substantial tea, of fresh stewed eels, for a change.

The walk was pleasant and they talked of all sorts of things, lost in each other's company as young lovers have done for centuries. Towards the end of the walk though, he was concerned that she seemed a little breathless and weary with her unaccustomed exertion. Gallantly he suggested she continue walking ahead when his shoe needed refastening, as he would soon catch her up with her slower pace. Catch her up he did, but to his dismay, she fell at that moment and breathed her last. The posy of flowers he had picked to surprise her when he stopped to refasten his shoe fell to the ground from his hand.

A Fenland Giant

Fenland folk are fond of recounting the tale of a mythical giant. This giant's name was Tom Hickathrift and he lived with his mother. Nobody knew who the father was and Tom's mother was certainly not going to revel his identity. Tom grew to be very large, but also very lazy. He made the excuse that he had outgrown his strength, but his mother scalded him and forced him to go and work for a farmer who wanted grain transported to Kings Lynn. He was to be paid a week's wages for each trip, since the way was dangerous and the safer detour took at least a couple of days' journey in each direction. Tom didn't think much to that, working for a whole week, so decided to take the short cut.

Driving the old ox cart full of grain along the narrow Fenland track, he heard a thunderous roar and the ground shook beneath his feet as he hopped down. The folk at the last hamlet had warned of a huge giant ogre who was terrorising the neighbourhood and stealing whatever he wanted. Tom had just smiled and thanked them for their entertaining tale without really believing it. It seemed a lot more real now and Tom Hickathrift prepared to defend his precious cargo. Not having a weapon and little he could use from the wayside, he heaved and tilted up the side of the cart and pulled at the cartwheel with his prodigious strength. His biceps bulged as it came off with the axle still attached. The ox snorted in distress, not knowing what was happening and panicking at the approaching thunderous footsteps. Separating the wheel from the axle, he held them as a shield and club.

The giant ogre appeared from around the bend, furious and surprised that anyone should oppose him. Lumbering towards Tom, his huge arms and solid fists whirling, he was startled to see his opponent spin the cartwheel. His great long shaggy hair caught into it as it spun and

Bury St Edmunds Abbey gateway. The miraculous martyr and saint, King Edmund, was eventually interred here.

rendered him helpless and the axle club that Tom laid about him reshaped his head. Tom had soon killed him and thought he ought to have a snooze after such exertions. He awoke to find the formerly frightened villagers gathered around him and the body of the dead giant. They thanked him profusely and gave him so much to eat and drink that he spent another day sleeping that off. Finally, they helped him to put the waggon back together again and off he went to deliver his load by the short route. On his return, he took his wages but never said what had happened, so while he was paid each trip for a week's work, it only took him a couple of days, leaving plenty of time for sleeping and eating. Eventually the story did get out and it can be seen pictured on the plasterwork of a building in Saffron Walden. Tom himself occupies an eight-foot grave in Terrington St Clement churchyard.

A Martyred King

Most people have heard of King Edmund being martyred for his Christian faith by the Danes, but few stop to wonder why he was singled out. After all, in most places they were happy for local populations to follow their own religions while the Vikings carried on their own Heathen rites. Some say that a shipwrecked Dane called Ragnar Lodbrok once came to the court of King Edmund and was treated well there as an honoured guest. However, he quarreled with a huntsman called Beorn, who murdered him and buried the corpse in a forest. However, the victim's dog lead Edmund's men to the murder scene and Beorn was set adrift in a small boat. Luckily for him, it drifted across the North Sea, where he found a welcome with his victim's sons, Ivar the Boneless and Ubba. Rather than admit what had happened (rules about giving and receiving hospitality were very important to both Saxon and Dane) he said that he had been cruelly mistreated and had narrowly escaped with his life, after his friend, their father had been executed by King Edmund. Hence when they invaded England in 870, his new friends made a point of hunting down King Edmund.

It is said that Edmund hid beneath Goldbrook Bridge at Hoxne and a bridal couple crossing it spotted the glint of his armour and betrayed him. He was captured and is said to have placed a curse on the bridge, which has resulted in couples who are on their way to be wed avoiding crossing it to this day.

The defeated king was taken away (some believe to Bradfield St Clare) and tied to a tree. Refusing to renounce his faith, as an example to his people, he was shot full of arrows. Finally, his head was struck off and thrown into Wayland Wood. A remnant of this once mighty forest can still be found near Watton and later became the scene of the Babes in the Wood story from nearby Griston Hall. Edmund's followers came searching for the head and were guided by a wolf's howling to where it lay. As they approached, the wolf loped off and they were able to reunite the head with its body in a chapel at Hellesdon, outside Norwich.

Eventually, the martyr's relics were transferred to the great Abbey of Beodricesworth, which became renamed Bury St Edmunds. Various miracles were associated with it and the head was said to have miraculously rejoined the body. A sacrilegious cleric doubted this and tugged at the body. He suffered a heart attack on the spot. A woman was employed to occasionally trim the fingernails and it is said that the body did not decompose. How much of this story was generated by those who grew rich on the pilgrimages made to the site is open to question, but there is not doubting the popularity and subsequent supernatural presence of this martyred king.

Goldbrook Bridge, Hoxne. After the betrayal of King Edmund, It is still thought to be unlucky for a bridal party to cross it.

The Murderous Nun

As can be expected, the great monastery and abbey have become a major part of Bury's identity. A brown monk and grey nun haunt the ruins, particularly at 11pm on 24 February each year. The monk is thought to be Brother Bernard and the nun, Maude Carew, a friend of Queen Margaret, who had decided to retire to the priory in 1447 and take holy vows. However, King Henry VI and his Queen arrived before she could reach that stage and she persuaded Maude to take part in a plot against Humphrey, the Duke of Gloucester. Cardinal Beaufort was also recruited to supply and teach Maude how to use a deadly poison against Humphrey. Maude accomplished the murder, but was careless in handling the deadly poison and died along with Humphrey. Brother Bernard, a former friend, found her and deduced what had happened. In cursing Maude to eternal unrest he too was condemned to wander, as well as the treacherous Queen Margaret. A monk is also said to haunt a bungalow on Malthouse Lane, on the former site of St Saviour's Hospice, where the Duke of Gloucester was murdered.

The abbey's high altar is thought by some to be directly on the St Michael's Ley Line, stretching from St Michael's Mount, Cornwall to the Norfolk coast. Many old towns and cities seem to have their own 'secret tunnel' stories, although many turn out to be ancient sewers, cellars, or, in Bury St Edmunds' case, chalk mines akin to the famous public ones at Grimes Graves near Brandon. Having said that, they may still have been used as a secret means of travel between one building and another, for lovers' assignations or criminal activity. Certainly, shopkeepers in Abbeygate Street have witnessed ghosts floating across their cellars. These same cellars were once communal before being separated into individual businesses by brickwork.

A Story in a Nutshell

The Nutshell is famous as probably the smallest licensed public house in England. Customers squeeze between a plethora of collected relics to get to the bar, but a third-floor bedroom has its own relic; that of the frequently sited ghost of a young boy who is said to have been murdered there. A severe drop in temperature often accompanies his appearance.

The Nutshell, Bury St Edmunds – the smallest pub in England – where some curious ghosts can be found.

Many other Bury St Edmunds buildings have reported hauntings, including: the storeroom at the John Menzies shop on Buttermarket; the Guildhall Street Conservative Club; and a house in Kings Road. Liturgical chanting was once heard by a cleaner in St Andrews Street and a ghostly nurse was once spotted at the old hospital at St Mary's. The Manor House Museum is said to have a Civil War soldier haunting the garden.

I Smell Ghosts!

A house in College Street in Bury St Edmunds has a rarer, but not unique, form of haunting; that of smell. It has often been said that a slight whiff of a particular smell, from baking bread to sea air, unlocks a host of memories and associations. In 1973, Andrew Abbott and his daughter Gillian told the *Bury Free Press* of the old-fashioned type of perfume they sometimes smelt in the house. They assumed it was from an elderly lady ghost seen walking about in what had been the servants' quarters on the top floor. Their description matched someone who had once worked there.

A Spirit in the Bar

People having a drink in Cupola House, Bury St Edmunds may think they have had a little too much when the lady at the end of the bar suddenly vanishes. Staff assure them that this is a regular spooky occurrence. The seventeenth-century building was once home to Daniel Defoe, author of *Robinson Crusoe* and *Moll Flanders* and also boasts a grey, lady ghost. One landlady once went to change a barrel in the cellar, but found it and the gas bottle were full. Trudging back upstairs she found that the pump still didn't work. Returning to the cellar, she found that the gas was now empty and 'something' appeared to be stopping her from lifting it up. The beer in question was a lager, so maybe it was the ghost of a real-ale drinker playing a prank.

Frightful Fornham Road

The Abbeyfords' car showroom (previously Mann Egerton's) had trouble getting cleaners to work in the evenings. Strange noises and uncanny feelings may have contributed, but the clocks running backwards would have meant their shift never finished! These strange occurances may have been linked to the fact that there was a burial ground in the area. Firemen in the old fire station that once stood further along that road also told of a mysterious figure who hovered near their beds.

The Faceless Man

Two boys were playing in a small strip of woodland adjacent to the Horringer Road, in 1970. A man approached, carrying a bag and walking stick and wearing a dark suit and bowler hat. It was what was beneath the hat that was disturbing though. Or rather, what was not beneath the hat. The boys reported that there was just an oval white shape where his face should have been.

The 'Late' Passengers

The sad ghosts of a wounded Crimean War soldier and the girl who nursed him can sometimes be seen underneath the gloomy railway arches near Mustow Street and the Bury St Edmunds railway station. The soldier was killed on the spot, stabbed by the girl's father, as they were trying to elope. The murderer was hanged and she ended up in a mental institution, demented by the loss of her happiness that was cut so violently short.

The Screaming Skull

The Red Barn murder at Polstead in Suffolk is a particularly notorious case and is a tale of another elopement that went horribly wrong. In the early nineteenth century Maria Marten was the lover of twenty-three-year-old William Corder. It seems likely that she was the unmarried mother of a child, Thomas Henry, fathered by a Mr Matthews. Matthews paid Corder's mother, Annie, to bring the boy up as her own, a practice not uncommon in days when illegitimacy carried great shame. William told Maria's parents and others that they were going off to Ipswich to get married and when he reappeared after several weeks without his 'wife', said that Maria had gone on to London. However, one night, Maria's mother had a prophetic dream (or some particularly vivid suspicions) and ordered her husband to go dig in the corner of the Red Barn. There he found the remains of Maria and the hunt was on for William Corder. He was eventually caught and brought to trial in Bury St Edmunds. Sentenced to hang on Monday 11 August 1828 at Bury goal, his execution attracted a crowd of over 5,000 people wanting to see the gory spectacle. Victorian melodrama plays were enacted and lurid 'penny dreadful' newsheets, telling the gruesome story, sold. It is estimated that approximately 1.5million copies of the 'broadside ballad' were also sold.

It has been suggested that Maria had made a tryst to meet William at the Red Barn on the afternoon of 17 May 1827, where she told him she was pregnant and had brought some clothes with her so that they could go away together. She is reported as having already lost one baby at birth, born at Sudbury and also fathered by Corder. She had also previously accused him of stealing some money sent by Mr Matthews for the upkeep of his child. Perhaps it was his fear of being found out that finally convinced him to kill Maria, as he shot, stabbed, strangled and buried her in the Red Barn. It is thought that he may have also been guilty of another crime in his early teens, when Sam 'Beauty' Smith was sentenced to transportation for the theft of a pig. Some said it was William who actually committed the crime, but he let Sam take the blame.

A death mask of William's face was made and can be seen alongside a grisly book about the trial that is bound with part of William's skin from the dissection by the County Surgeon, George Creed in the twelfth-century Moyes Hall Museum. It was common in those days for executed criminals' bodies to be given for medical research.

Corder's skeleton was re-assembled and used as a teaching aid in the West Suffolk Hospital. It came to the attention of Dr John Kilner, who worked there in the 1870s. He had a ghoulish

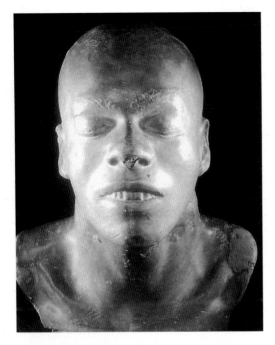

William Corder's death mask is displayed at Moyse Hall Museum, Bury St Edmunds. The museum also contains his pistols, scalp and a trial book bound in his skin.

'A Correct View of the Red Barn. Polstead Barn was destroyed by fire some years since

A drawing of Red Barn, Polstead, the Maria Marten murder scene before it burnt down. Also shown is the cottage of her parents.

collection of skulls at his home, but desired this special one for his collection that he used to further his study of phrenology. There used to be a particular study of whether criminals' skulls were of a different form to more law-abiding citizens. Secretly, he exchanged the skull for another, smuggling out William's in his capacious doctor's medical bag. But the skull brought its own curse and Dr Kilner was subject to horrifying dreams and noises of heavy breathing and screaming. A ghostly hand shattered the glass case in which the skull was displayed and in abject terror the doctor persuaded his friend, Mr Hopkins, to get the skull a decent burial. Mr Hopkins himself twisted his ankle while carrying the skull, causing it to fall to the ground and be screamed at by a passing lady acquaintance. Thankfully, when burial was completed, the screaming stopped.

Many people went to view the Red Barn in Polstead and locals said that it sometimes glowed blood red in the night. Eventually, the barn glowed red from a fire that destroyed it.

The vicarage in Polstead is haunted though. Reverend Hayden Foster and his wife Margo had a remarkable experience when they lived there in 1978. Less than a week after moving in Margo awoke in the middle of the night to see all the recently decorated walls peeling and feeling as if she was being strangled. Some villagers have talked of a seeing the spectre of a Polstead boy who was murdered by a monk and, indeed, many have seen whole processions of monks crossing the road. After moving out the Fosters found that the place had been exorcised of evil spirits at least twice in its history, going back as far as the early 1800s. Proof, perhaps, that some exorcisms don't work.

A dramatic appearance

William Wilkins created the beautiful Theatre Royal in Bury St Edmunds in 1819, but it had cost him a lot of money by 1830 and he died before it fulfilled its true potential. He also worked on the National Gallery in London. The theatre closed in 1843, reopening in 1845 under a new owner, William Abington.

Visitors today can see the fine architecture and Regency styling restored by the National Trust, but how many notice the sad man in a grey suit? Although some believe it is a lovelorn 'stage door Johnny' trying to find the actress whose passion was curtailed by her sudden death, others like to think that the ghost is William, returning to see the shows he never managed to produce.

Strange happenings in Bradfield St George

Back in the 1920s, two chaps from Bradfield St George had been visiting the Theatre Royal and returned on their motorbikes to Hall Farm. On the way they had seen a glow in the distance, over to the west. Motorbike fuel tanks were not large in those days, so they had stopped to refuel before making off towards where they thought a barn fire must be blazing. Their dog barked furiously and they were amazed to see bright light streaming from the windows of their farmhouse. It was not a reflection. Going inside, all was dark and when they came back outside, the light from the window and the glow in the distance were gone. Nobody else saw anything and no fires were reported. Could it have been an early close encounter with a UFO, or was there another explanation? We shall never know, but it isn't the only odd thing to have happened in Bradfield St George.

Every now and again, someone walking along a particular stretch of road on the way to Rougham sees a large Georgian mansion, complete with flower garden. A complete school party visiting the area and led by teacher Ruth Wynne (daughter of the Vicar of Rougham), saw it in 1926 , but couldn't relocate it when they came back the following spring. A local man called Robert Palfrey saw it from a field on Kingshall Street in the summer of 1860, but the next minute, after he had climbed down the ladder of the haystack he was working on, he could no longer see it either. He was followed by his great grandson James Cobbold in 1912 who had the same experience while helping a local butcher make deliveries by pony cart. No one else is able to see this mirage for long and the land on which the barn is seen to be standing is just an empty field … there is no record of any such building in the area.

Arsenic in Acton

Catherine Foster of Acton had only been married to her husband for three weeks in 1846 when she killed him. She was just seventeen, felt that she would be happier back working in service and later said that although he was kind, she did not love him and had married due to pressure from her mother. Dr Jones of Long Melford had assumed the death to be caused by English

There used to be a begging rhyme sung around St Valentine's Day that is associated with Acton:

> *Good morning to your Valentine, Curl your locks as I curl mine*
> *Two before and two behind, Good morning to your Valentine.*
> *I only come but once a year, Pray give me some money as I stand here*
> *Piece of cake or glass of wine, Good morning to your Valentine.*
> *Rural courtship didn't always go so smooth – see the story about Acton.*

Cholera, but after an inquest, a post mortem was requested. Traces of arsenic were found when the body exhumed and examined in Acton churchyard. The eight-year-old brother of the murder victim recalled at the trial how he had seen Catherine put a black powder into some dumplings and that some hens had died after eating parts of these.

The jury at Bury St Edmunds only took fifteen minutes to find her guilty and 10,000 spectators witnessed her hanging. She was the first criminal to be buried at the gaol and the last woman to be hanged in Bury. Her husband was reburied in Acton churchyard, but is still said to wander abroad in November each year, the time of his death.

Strangely enough, he shares the churchyard (or possibly a nearby site underneath the church chancel) with that of a convicted murderer; unusual that he should be buried in consecrated ground. Charles Drew shot his father six times in Long Melford. There was a dispute about the small allowance he was to be given, due to the bad company he kept. Having hidden the gun in a hollow tree at Liston, Charles went to London to deal with his father's will, which would have made him a wealthy man. Having found that a warrant had been issued for his arrest, he went on the run, but was captured and sent for trial from Newgate Assizes to Bury. The twenty-five year old was found guilty on 27 March 1740 and hanged. His older sister Mary Drew was married to the Revd Charles Umfreville, who secretly buried the murderer at the church.

Inheritances seem to be ill fated in Acton. A certain miser, William Jennings died there, without leaving a will, in 1798. The Chancery case dragged on until the 1880s and is the likely source of the fictional Chancery case of Jarndyce and Jarndyce in Charles Dickens' *Bleak House*.

Rigor Mortis in Rushbrooke Hall

Within four miles of Bury, the enigmatic Rushbrooke Hall, dating from the mid-sixteenth century, has a white lady ghost, murdered either by her husband or others, depending on which version of the story you believe. She is seen floating around, which is quite appropriate since she was drowned in the moat after being flung from an upper storey.

A Romantic Ghost

The Ipswich *Evening Star* reported the case of a landlady, Mrs White, of the Royal Oak pub in Stowmarket. She spoke of a ghostly man waving to her in her bedroom mirror. She said that, 'at first I was petrified, but then felt absolutely wonderful and had no worries about the dentist!' She recalled he had long hair and was wearing an old-style nightshirt. He had also been spotted another time by Mrs White's mother and daughter and gave them a wave. The new owners of the pub have also noted that their dog starts barking non-stop in the direction of the pool table.

If you think that last tale was a 'fairy story' you had better skip this paragraph: Suffolk doesn't have many tales of the wee folk, but in the early 1800s many 3ft-tall creatures in glistening clothes were reported to be seen dancing in a ring. The location was a meadow between Stowmarket and Bury St Edmunds.

It is not the only tale of little folk in this area. Ralph of Coggeshall wrote in 1210 of a fairy changeling child at nearby Dagworth. Malekin, as she was called, frequented the castle home of

The Oak, Stowmarket. Wave to the romantic ghost there, but only if you are a lady.

Osbern of Bradwell, talking in the local dialect or in Latin to the priest. She told them that she had been kidnapped from her mother by fairies in a field and returned seven years later. She kept mainly invisible, except to one friendly servant girl who left out food for her, but was said to be heard to speak by many.

Bewildering Buxhall

Near to Stowmarket, in the village of Buxhall, there is a house named Rawmarsh that has been converted from three cottages adjoining a small chapel and graveyard. One eccentric lady owner used to take a bath in her back yard, until one day she was found drowned in it. Since then, successive owners seem to have bad luck in their health or marriage.

One room, used as a study, would drip from the ceiling, but there would be no corresponding wet patch on the floor. An incident on the stairs leading from the study 'froze' one lady rigid while she watched the latch on an upstairs door move about by itself.

The Wool Combers

Many people are aware that some of Suffolk's most picturesque towns owe their original wealth to the wool trade and the Flemish weavers, who fled religious persecution in the seventeenth century, to come here. (Unfortunately, shortly after their arrival many were caught up in the English Civil Wars.) Kersey, Lavenham and Hadleigh are but three places that enjoyed a boom period of building and development then.

Hadleigh's name is derived from Old English words for a 'heather clearing' (*hæth* and *lēah*) and there used to be a grand annual procession of a lamb, plus an effigy of Bishop Blaize, the patron saint of wool combers, in the town. Before wool can be spun and woven it has to be combed with great spiked brushes. It all sounds quite quaint and folksy until you realise why Bishop Blaize was selected as the appropriate saint of wool combers; his martyrdom was achieved by being torn to pieces by combs. Incidentally, one of the church bells that would have rung out in celebration is believed to be England's oldest, dating back to the fourteenth century. It is rather unusual, because the inscription runs backwards due to a mistake made in the bell foundry.

A Weaving Goblin

Talking of those weaving communities brings us to a Suffolk version of an internationally known folk tale. A girl whose mother has told the King that she is a wonderful spinner, in an effort to marry her off is put to work, imprisoned in a tower. If she cannot spin all the flax brought in to cover the floor each day for three days, her head will be the forfeit. If she survives, she will be his Queen and work no more.

Crying and despairing, she perceives a small goblin in the corner, who says he will help. He is able to spin the entire huge amount of flax by magic. His offer comes with conditions though. If she cannot guess his name in three nights, he will take her away to be his bride and unlike the King he is hideously ugly. She guesses wrongly for the first two nights, while a friend is away trying to find out the correct name. He returns just in time to call out to her window that he heard a voice by a fire in the forest singing 'Nimmie nimmie not, my name is Tom Tit Tot.'

She proclaims the name to the goblin's disgust and he disappears. The King comes in, delighted that she has completed the task and proposes marriage. Being sensible though, the girl rejects him in favour of the friend whom saved her life by finding out the goblin's name. After all, who would want a husband who once threatened to cut off your head for not working hard enough?

Flight From Fear at Rougham

Suffolk was covered in airbases during the Second World War, some temporary and others more permanent. It is unsurprising that the high mortality rates of those gallant young aircrews that flew from them, has resulted in a ghost or two lingering on. Such a case is the control tower of Rougham Airfield, where many flights were sent on missions but failed to return. While spending some time here, setting up military exhibitions with his son, Mr X has experienced some strange goings-on. After locking the top of the control tower on leaving, the pair heard footsteps above their heads when they had moved downstairs. Thinking a helper had been left behind and locked in, they went back upstairs, unlocked and looked around. There was no one there. Similar incidents have also occurred including an investigator who saw a Second World War pilot, complete with goggles, helmet and gas mask looking out from the window. He made a sharp exit.

Not a Picture of Innocence

Many important families have their feuds and in the nineteenth century, at Yaxley Hall, Yaxley, Henrietta Nelson took a positive dislike to some of hers. Knowing that the family would inherit the place when she died she had a massive mausoleum built for her before her death (rather than be buried in the vault of the family she so despised) that completely spoiled the view from the Hall. She died in 1816, at the age of eight-two, having suffered a fall.

A few generations later, her personal mausoleum was knocked down during alterations, her remains moved to the family vault in the church and her ghost started to walk. Unusually, it seemed to attach itself to a painting of her and appeared in whichever room the ancestral painting was hung. Maybe it was an attempt to let the family know which ancestor was haunting them. Eventually, the family sold it, but it was stolen from the new owner in 1995 and has never been recovered. Let us hope Henrietta is giving the burglar a hard time.

This is not the only case of cursed paintings in Suffolk. A pair of paintings, of a nun and a mother superior, hang in Coldham Hall, a sixteenth-century, twelve-bedroomed house at Stanningfield. They are said to bring bad luck to anyone who takes them down and are covenanted to be sold with the house each time it changes hands.

The people who may risk the effect of the curse nowadays could be the German supermodel Claudia Schiffer or her husband Matthew Vaughn, the film producer, who bought the house when they wed, in May 2005. The ghost of another nun, Penelope Rookwood, who used to spend time at the house during summer months, may also keep them company. Penelope was a member of the family descended from Sir Robert Rookwood who built the original house in 1575.

The Green Children of Woolpit

It is thought that the name Woolpit may be derived from the words 'wolf pit', harking back to the times when these animals still roamed our county. It would have been deep, probably with spikes at the bottom and a disguised covering. However, it wasn't the howl of wolves the villagers heard one day, but that of children, one boy and one girl. They had fallen to the bottom of the pit and were crying out for help. On helping them out, the villagers realised with amazement that their skins were tinged with green and they spoke an unfamiliar language. Uncertain what to do, they took them before the local head man, who suggested that they were probably no different to children anywhere and that a local widow should take them in, feed them and love them at the village's expense.

She did take them in and showed them genuine affection, but they remained frightened and would not eat any of the food she tried to tempt them with. The young boy became weak and ill and nobody could find out who they were or where they came from. Eventually, they saw some peas being brought back from the fields and grabbed some, stuffing them into their hungry mouths with joy – pods and all. It seemed that they did not recognise vegetables that had been cooked and were not used to meat either. Kindly neighbours brought other raw green vegetables for them to eat, but it was too late for the lad, who succumbed and died.

The girl cried for her dead brother for a long time; the only familiar person who could speak her language was now gone. As she grew older and stronger, she started to try some of the villagers' other food, but always showed a preference for raw vegetables. Her green hue faded. She gradually learnt the local language too, but by then her discovery in the wolf pit was a distant childhood memory. All that she could recall was that she had come from a place called St Martins Land. She and her brother had gone exploring down a hole that eventually led to a tunnel. They had become hopelessly lost, until they saw a glimmer of light. That was the sunshine lighting the bottom of the pit in which they had been found.

The girl grew up and was employed as a maid in a local large household. A young man visiting there on business took a shine to her and returned to his home in Kings Lynn with her where they married and had several children.

The story was originally told in a document by William of Newburgh and relates to the early 12th century.

Incidentally, returning to a canine theme, a Woolpit farmer once thought a calf was stuck in a pit, but it turned out to be a wolf. When he returned with his gun it had disappeared. Might it have been Black Shuck the phantom devil dog? In the 19th century he was reported as having caught a man and telling him he would be dead soon. The man died the following night, whether of fright or not, no one could tell. We shall meet Black Shuck some more on the East Coast, but it is unusual for him to be credited with speech.

He is not the only strange beast to be found in the parish. St Mary's church, part of which dates back to the 1200s, incorporates an earlier Saxon cross, the Shrine of Our Lady of Woolpit and a Healing Well. Beside the pulpit is a Woodwose – a wild man figure found in various churches around Suffolk. He is kept company by heraldic beasts on the pew ends and over two hundred angels carved into the double hammerbeam roof. Twenty-one examples of this type of roof are found in Suffolk, which is two thirds of the known total of thirty-one such roofs in the world. If you are lucky enough to visit the place, feel the tops of the pillars on the outside of the priests' door. The shells of the oysters from the mason's lunch are integrated into the plaster. That doesn't mean he was rich – oysters were common fare for poor people before they gained their modern exclusivity.

The Woolpit sign showing the mysterious green children and a wolf.

31

The Suffolk Miracle

One might be forgiven for thinking that this story is about some other holy place or sainted relics. In fact, it concerns a song first published in 1711 and called the *Suffolk Miracle*. It is a remarkably complete version of what folklorists categorise as 'night visiting songs'. This song contains all the classic folk song features, in its twenty-eight verses, and is the archetype by which all others of the genre are compared. As far as it is known, it has only been commercially recorded once, by Suffolk folk singer John Goodluck and he edited out two verses. It is believed that the song was based on a story already in circulation at the time.

Young William is broken-hearted at being separated from his true love and visits her late at night on horseback. Tapping on her window, she comes down and greets him with joy, accepting his offer of a pillion horseback ride by moonlight. On the ride she notices he looks pale and wan and ties her handkerchief around his head to keep him from the cold. Arriving back at her uncle's house, she rushes in to tell him the good news of William's return, while he puts the horse away in the stable. Her uncle exclaims with horror that this is not possible, since William died and was buried some months ago in a neighbouring town, but they chose not to tell her. On her insistence the corpse is exhumed from the grave and the griefstruck lover sees his body lying there in the coffin, her handkerchief still tied around his head.

Strange Bedfellows in Great Bricett

There used to be a pair of dilapidated cottages, which have since been demolished, standing near the village post office; a single step that once led to the path survives in the roadside bank. Around 1900, some itinerant Irish labourers working in the area were housed in the cottages. As was often the practice those days, two men had to share one double bed. During the night, one woke up cold to find his bed partner had hogged all the covers and he rolled towards the centre of the bed to recover them. What he saw there brought him fully, stark staring awake. His yell woke his comrade too and they both witnessed a ghostly old lady occupying the centre of the bed.

A Short Coach Ride

The chance to ride in a proper coach and four may be a treat for many, but don't think of boarding the one in Acton though! It starts from the gates of Acton Place and only goes as far as Nursery Corner ... then it disappears! A couple fled their home on Barrow Hill, Acton when ghostly footsteps followed them around and doors opened and closed of their own accord. Also, there is reputed to be a treasure chest hidden by Wimbell Pond. Anyone getting too close to it is frightened away with a ghastly cry of 'That is mine!'

The Crown Inn of Bildeston dates back to the 1400s and was an important coaching inn, but I do not think I will try there either. A guest was paralysed in a room there in 1977 while his companion slumbered on and similar things have happened to other people since then. Room 6 is said to be haunted and staff and guests see a man in a three-cornered hat near the front door, as well as a spectral lady sometimes drifting across the courtyard. Whether she is the same

Bildeston Crown Inn claims to be the site of a number of hauntings.

redhead who accosts men in the toilets is unknown. Most curious of all are the children playing with a music box which can sometimes be heard. They never frightened off the notorious East End gangsters the Kray twins, who used to enjoy a drink there, but who would? However, a more recent ghost seen in the bar is of a man in a baggy brown suit, wagging his finger as if in argument. Could he be one of their unlucky associates?

Down the road at Lindsey White Rose a malevolent spirit was blamed for causing a fire, among some other odd events.

The Sacrilegious Sacristan

One can still see the Austin Friars' Priory in the beautiful village of Clare - named after a Celtic root word meaning mild or pleasant water and no doubt referring to the river Stour which runs through it. It was established by the patronage of Richard de Clare, the Earl of Gloucester in 1248. Sadly, about two hundred years later standards had slipped and the Prior Galfridus seemed more concerned with storing up food and drink on earth than blessings in Heaven.

The sacristan, Hugh, had borrowed money using the treasures of the priory as surety and worried how to cover up his sacrilege. An answer was at hand when a stranger in a dark, heavily

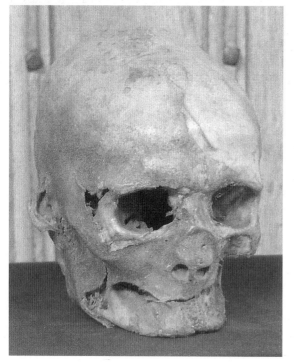

Above: *Clare Priory, once home to a corrupt Sacristan.*

Left: *Simon of Sudbury's skull – Archbishop of Canterbury and victim of Peasants' Revolt.*

hooded habit suggested that he saved candles that had been left to burn, trim them and sell them again. It seemed a great idea, except for the condition added by the stranger: the first candle taken must be preserved, since if it were ever to burn, his soul would be forfeit.

You can guess the ending. One night the sacristan had to visit a cellar and took up the preserved candle. Helping himself to some wine, he dozed off. He awoke to a feint spluttering, as the last drips of wax from the cursed candle burnt away. His fellow brothers awoke to a piercing scream and ran to the source, only to find his dead body, the face horribly twisted and contorted.

Simon of Sudbury's Skull

A gruesome relic of the Peasants' Revolt of 1381 is kept in a special niche in the vestry wall of St Gregory's church, Sudbury. It is the skull of Simon of Sudbury, Archbishop of Canterbury, credited with inventing an early form of poll tax. It was a different type of 'pole' that this head found itself paraded on, in front of the marching mob until the army put them to rout. Mysterious sounds and footsteps have been heard, so maybe his body, buried in the cathedral, seeks to be reunited. What he will not be reunited with is his teeth, since they were sold off one by one by an old cleric as souvenir relics.

Some of the rioters were rounded up in Sudbury's Market Square and massacred by the military, despite a promise of an amnesty. Today the place is more peaceful, overseen by the statue of Thomas Gainsborough the artist, whose house down the road forms a museum of his life and works.

There is a curious sight too at one of Sudbury's other fine churches, St Peter and St Paul's. A large woodwose carving can be found there. In common with other carved stone woodwose figures to be found in other Suffolk churches (including Yoxford, Badingham, Framlingham, Yaxley and Orford) he has a vertical striped body, lots of hair and carries a club. Nobody can be sure what they represent: a wild man; demon; or nature spirit? In many other Suffolk churches one can find many enigmatic green man figures; heads that sprout vegetation from the nose, mouth or ears. They have become very popular in recent years, with lots of modern recreations being produced, but for original foliate figures try looking inside or outside churches in Clare, Thurston, Cavendish, Hacheston, Dennington, Little and Great Waldingfield, Metfield and Grundisburgh to name but a few locations.

You can still see part of a Dominican friary, founded in 1272, which is now a house in Friary Street, Sudbury. Somewhat unsurprisingly, a monk is said to haunt it.

Just outside Sudbury, on the Essex border is a place called Ballingdon Hill. According to a document in Canterbury Cathedral, on 26 September 1449 two dragons fought overhead. One was the black dragon of Suffolk and the other the reddish spotted dragon of Essex. The battle was inconclusive and the dragons returned to their own counties. Several counties have dragon stories, but rarely is one found with such an exact date to it.

Bures, a village that lies in both Suffolk and Essex has a dragon story, predating the Ballingdon one, from 1405. It did the usual things that dragons are supposed to do – eating sheep and terrifying the locals until it was frightened away by volleys of arrows directed at it by Richard de Waldegrave and his men. The scaly hide and pointed teeth were seen no more in the district, apart from a nearby church wall painting in Wiston (also known as Wissington). Wiston and the appropriately named Wormingford are both over the border in Essex.

Right: *A Woodwose, SS Peter and Paul's church, Sudbury. Is there a possibility that, like the Green Man, Woodwose is a symbol of vigorous natural growth and fecundity? During the night before May Day young men and women would go into woods and gather May (allegedly!) to leave at people's doors. They would return later with this rhyme:*

Now we've been rambling all the night, and some part of the day.
And now we're returning back again. We've brought you a branch of May.
A branch of May we've brought you here, and at your door it shall stand.
It is but a sprout, but tis well budded out, by the work of the good Lords hand.
Arise, arise you dairy maids, arouse from your drowsy dream
And step into your dairy house for a sup of your sweet cream.
And if not a sup of your sweet cream, then a jug of your brown beer.
And if I live and flourish on, I'll call on another year.

Below: *The old Dominican Friary in Sudbury.*

East Bergholt Bell Cage, at the heart of Constable Country.

Before we leave Bures, mention must be made of the Skellet Hole of Burgh Road. In 1892, the rector, no less, informed Lady Gurdon (a contributor to the *Folk-Lore Magazine*) of the local bogey woman who washed her utensils (including a skellet or skillet) in a watery channel beneath the road. He also spoke of a ghost giving its name to Whitefoot Lane.

Ghosts in a Cemetery?

Given the nature of the places, it is remarkable that ghosts are not more often associated with cemeteries. A spook hunter from Hadleigh followed up reports of a black figure standing at the top of Hadleigh Cemetery. Fully equipped with an infra-red video camera and EMF (Electro Magnetic Field) meter, he waited until 2.30 a.m. before hearing footsteps and seeing a luminous ball of light moving towards him. Nothing registered on the instruments before it disappeared. He waited until dawn and was rewarded by a sighting of the dark shape only fifteen yards away from where he was sat. However, it vanished as he approached.

Caged Bells

Visitors to Constable Country frequently visit the charming village of East Bergholt and are drawn to look at the wooden cage, which contains the bells, in the churchyard. Numerous accidents and incidents occurred, including the death of one man who was crushed, when the locals tried to hang the bells in the church, so it was thought better to keep them outside. Just opposite is a haunted Benedictine convent: St Mary's Abbey.

During the Second World War the convent was used to house a troop of soldiers. Each night, at around 10.50 p.m., in the room they used as a Sergeants' Mess, the temperature would suddenly drop and the door would open on its own. A young soldier in another room was visited one night and after some unearthly, icy hands had touched his face, his hair was found to have turned white in the morning.

Burrough green children – will they come down and play with you?

Bergholt means 'hill wood' from the Old English *beorg* or *berg* (hill) and *holt* (wood.) West Bergholt is ten miles away, across the Essex border.

Dismal Denham

The investigators from Suffolk & Norfolk Paranormal Investigations think that Denham, near Chevington, is Suffolk's most haunted village. With reason; they have identified eleven ghosts in and around the hall. A monk walks along an old footpath and a lady crosses a bridge, while another exits the church gate and a misty figure floats down the hill. The hill has 'cold spots' and a pair of red, staring eyes appear there. Another ghostly lady walks up a cottage path on the hill and yet another lady in Victorian clothes perambulates the gardens of the hall.

One of the investigators, Richard Keeble, originates from the village and was disturbed by the sound of chains dragging up the streets as a child. He has since come to believe that the sound is an echo from the past and is assocaited with a girl, accused of witchcraft, who was dragged along for all to see, before being hanged.

Other sightings include: the headless corpse of a farmworker who met a grisly end under the wheels of a waggon in the 1920s; and a former parson who makes the doors of the church, from which chanting emanates, slam, although no one is there. Maybe the music is made by a ghostly congregation of dead villagers who gather there.

Denham Hall itself (nowadays divided into flats) has its own phenomena, including: moving lights; footsteps; a disappearing bloodstain; and ghosts of two people and a dog.

Come Out to Play?

A charming piece of folklore ends our journey around West Suffolk: above the door of a school hall in Burrough Green is a pair of statues. They depict a boy and girl in early eighteenth-century dress. If you can watch at midnight, on the eve of May Day, they are said to come to life and dance and play on the village green.

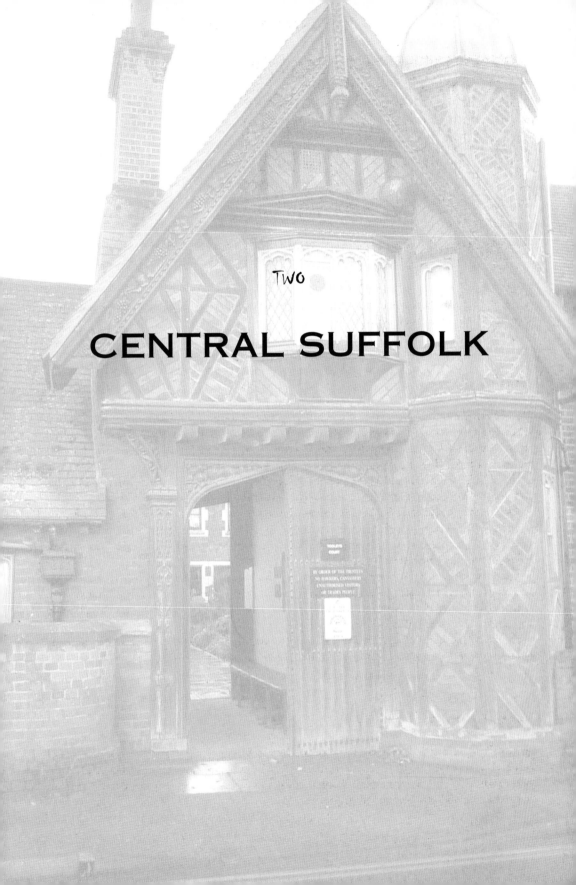

TWO

CENTRAL SUFFOLK

A Family Story

I have been extraordinarily lucky in being introduced convincingly to the subject of ghosts at a tender and impressionable age of about thirteen. The person who did the convincing was my mother, who had everything to lose by telling what had happened to her. She was a very straightforward, down-to-earth and disbelieving sort of person and very concerned lest the neighbours should think her odd in any way. We lived on a rough council estate road in Ipswich, where being thought of as 'different' was a positive disadvantage. If anyone else had told me such a tale at the time, I would have probably dismissed it as a wind up, a tall tale. But my mother was totally honest and would have been put at a great disadvantage if I had disobeyed her and blabbed the story while she was around, so I felt compelled to believe it.

Back in the 1930s she worked as a live-in cook for a branch of the Italian Zagni family. The name has been well known in Suffolk for over a century as the owners of Peters' Ice Creams, but my mother worked for a branch of the family who owned Zagni Asphalt, in Hutland Road, Ipswich. Apart from her, there was the master and mistress and their daughter Bonnie, who was in her twenties. The only other member of staff was a maid who came in to clean on a daily basis.

Mother described how one day she entered her long kitchen from the garden. At the other end of the kitchen she could see a man reading a newspaper, with his legs crossed and resting on the chair. She thought this was a bit 'off' because nobody entered the kitchen without the cook's say so in those days, either from courtesy or safety. However, not being particularly bothered, my mother (Phyllis Howe in those days) walked up the kitchen, musing that it might be a young man for Bonnie, who never seemed to have a boyfriend, despite being a lovely lady. But as she drew level with the man on her way into the main house, she felt something was not right and this was confirmed dramatically when he faded in front of her eyes.

Of course, she ran yelling into the house and between sobs told the mistress what she had seen. Calming her, her boss told her that it was an extraordinarily vivid description of her son-in-law. 'I didn't know you had one,' said mother. 'Oh yes, Bonnie was once married, for about a year, before your time here', was the reply.

Mother went on to describe how her daughter had a childhood sweetheart, whom she said she would marry when they were older. They went on to fall in love, but he caught tuberculosis; a fatal disease with little cure in those days. Despite that, they did marry and he came to live with them in Hutland Road. They even built a wooden hut in the garden so that he should get plenty of fresh air, which was a recommendation for those with TB. On warm summer nights he would sometimes sleep in the hut, so as not to keep the family awake with his coughing. In the morning he would come back into the house and pick up Mr Zagni's newspaper from the breakfast table. Inevitably, to keep out of the way, he would go and sit in the corner of the kitchen, characteristically with his legs folded up onto the chair. Sadly he died, the shed was taken down and his picture removed from the wall so as not to provide a constant sad reminder.

Mrs Zagni went and got the picture from a draw and showed it to my mother, but as the newspaper had obscured his face she could not positively identify him. Her employer had no doubt though from the description. 'You obviously have the gift of second sight, my dear,' she said gently. My mother tried to take this in, while the woman continued. 'You were not to know, but sometimes when you have your afternoon off, we hold a spiritualist seance here. Maybe you would like to join us sometime?' 'Not blooming likely!' was the spirited reply. The ghost was not seen again and a month or two after mother left to get married to my father, Ron Jennings.

Number 261 Landseer Road was built on old agricultural land. Shortly after she moved in she

Domestic work was a major source of employment in the last century.

came across the ghost of an old gentleman gazing across her living room. She said she wondered if he was the old farmer, coming to see what had happened to his land. He appeared twice more and on the third visit mother summoned up the courage to ask who he was and could she help him, but he faded and was seen no more.

Private Ghosts

As can be seen from the last story, hauntings are not limited to public buildings and may occur, wanted or not, in various private dwellings. There are houses with spooks in Bulwer Road (someone running upstairs), Eagle St (whispering on the stairs) and on the Chantry Estate (a grey-haired man with a red T-shirt) all of which have experienced manifestations. [The exact locations in Ipswich are not revealed to protect the privacy of the occupants.]

Mrs Amelia Cobb relates the sighting of a ghost at No. 53, St George's Street, where she lived as a young girl. It had been rebuilt over the ruins of a previous house that had burnt down. The lady who lived there died in the fire, reportedly trying to retrieve her moneybox from under the bed. Mrs Cobb remembers the bedclothes being pulled away from her, but never told anyone, since she didn't think she would be believed. She also mentioned a haunted house at the beginning of London Road, on the raised section reached by a flight of steps.

Some businesses prefer not to have their ghosts publicised while they are trading, such as the ex-Shanks' Bakery in St Helen's, which had a ghost upstairs. Evening cleaners at a doctors' surgery, near the town centre, are said to have seen a small child on the stairs. Some sightings of ghosts are hushed up at the time, but revealed later, such as the 1940s sighting of a lady photographer in the Rose Hill School assembly hall. That isn't the only haunted school. A policeman on patrol in his car one night near Chantry High School, around 1976, saw a man in a long overcoat emerge. Thinking he was about to apprehend an exiting burglar, he got out of the vehicle to give chase, when the man faded before his eyes. Unwisely he went back to the police station and told his colleagues what had happened and so became the butt of their jokes for a while.

Entertaining Ghosts

The Corn Exchange stands on the site of St Mildred's church, which may explain the presence of an ecclesiastical figure sometimes seen at the back of the basement film theatre. Of course, it may be more connected with the Court of Common Pleas that also stood there, since churchmen were often used as clerks because of their education. The ghost of a young boy has also been seen and years after this a small skeleton was found during alterations to the land.

Previously The Corn Exchange had been the largest and most prestigious place for me as a DJ to play. A commissionaire, named Jack, always had a ready smile, friendly word and held doors open for people when they were bringing in their equipment. He always reckoned he wanted to die on the job and loved being part of the entertainment industry.

Jack was forced to retire when he reached the appropriate age, but still came back to work casually. One night, after a show, when he had bid the departing audience a cheery goodnight, he sat down on a chair and died, in exactly the way he would have wished. One of the box-office ladies doesn't believe he has completely left the building though. He was always keen to play harmless practical jokes and it appears that his mischeivous spirit continues to do so, for instance, moving the reels of tickets she has just got out or lowering the swivel chair so that she cannot see above the counter!

There used to be another theatre ghost at the old Arts Repertory Theatre in Tower Street, which is now a bar. Actors would see a man in hat and coat looking up from the centre of the front stalls as they conducted afternoon rehearsals. He was always regarded as a good luck omen, as good reviews were given and full houses taken after his appearance. He acquired a number of names (Bill, Robert and Alfred, to name but a few), but it seems he failed to follow the actors to their new home at the Wolsey Theatre.

The Cracked Mirror and Dogs Head

In the early 1970s the Wolsey Room, part of the Plough Inn on the corner of Old Cattlemarket, Ipswich was run by a couple from Yorkshire called Jim and Doris Biddulph. Jim was nicknamed 'Ban em Biddulph' for his frequent habit of banning people, although he would let them back in after a week or two.

One day Doris suggested that he convert an old junk room into a bedroom for any of their relatives to stay in if they visited. He cleared, cleaned, tidied and decorated to create a pleasant room and brought in a bed, wardrobe and chest of drawers. The last thing he did as a finishing touch was to screw a mirror to the wall. Returning an hour or two later he found it had a large crack across one corner. Had the mirror been faulty, or was it simply a case of tightening the screws too much? He wasn't sure, but went and bought a replacement a couple of days later. He checked it over and made sure he didn't over tighten the screws, but within a day or two shattered pieces of the mirror lay on the floor. Puzzled, he tried other types of mirror: a freestanding mirror (this fell from where it stood and broke) and a wall mirror hung from a new piece of chain (a link snapped, depositing the mirror on the floor and cracking it). Eventually he gave up and joked about the 'mirror-cracker ghost' he must have in that room, despite never having seen anything ghostly himself. He did, however, mention that the room seemed colder than the rest of the building.

Years went by and managers changed several times, but still people would tell of strange goings-on in that room at the Plough. An electrician noted that his firm had been back to the small room upstairs at the back, because light bulbs kept popping, three times.

A new manangeress, Michelle (who used the room mainly for storage), adds a new twist to the tale. In December, Michelle was quite excited at the prospect of her boyfriend returning home from sea and moving in for their first Yule together. Her boyfriend had arrived as planned just before Christmas laden down with belongings. Getting to the top of the stairs he asked where to dump them and she had indicated the disused room. Pushing the door open, and with his hands full, he elbowed the light switch on. The bulb lit and then went out. When he leant back out of the doorway to call and tell her, he saw a shadowy figure retreating down the corridor and wondered whether he had done the right thing in agreeing to move in. She had not told him the other tales about that room until then, but perhaps Jim's many broken mirrors brought multiples of seven years' bad luck – this event was thirty years after the first!

There is one final addition to this tale that has occurred during the writing of this book. Michelle and her boyfriend got married and had a baby boy, who is now about two years old. He can now walk and talk as toddlers do, but when he passes the room in question he points and says, 'Man!' or 'Nasty Man!' Needless to say, at his tender age they have not told him anything about the story.

The Plough Inn is partly on Dogs Head Street and is named after another older pub, that has since been demolished, called the Dog's Head in a Pot. This strange name derives from the Flemish brewers and innkeepers who came over with their weaving countrymen in the 1600s. I was amused to find out later that 'Dog's Head in a Pot' is an old joke, and still a phrase used in Flemish dialect, meaning a slovenly household; the sign of a dog licking out a pot suggested that the house was too lazy to wash the dishes!

The Silent Street

Not far from the Plough Inn, there is a narrow road called Silent Street. With a busy port, it was inevitable that various diseases would be brought into Ipswich (with the exotic cargoes) and the town has had its share of plagues. In the 1700s the street was lined with tenement buildings, with the rooms on each floor rented out to different families. With many children sharing beds and poor sanitation, the slum-like conditions were ripe for disease to spread and

The Plough Inn, Ipswich – home of the continuing Mirror Cracker Ghost story.

an outbreak of smallpox killed everyone in the street except two children who were sent away to the country early on. Bodies were hastily buried in a plague pit together at nearby St Nicholas' church. There wasn't enough time or labour available to provide separate coffins and funerals.

With the buildings empty and people wary of using them, one landlord went broke and the others pulled down the properties and created a new, modern and more hygienic place to live. But the history of the area was too powerful to forget and the name given during that terrible time has stuck – Silent Street.

All Around the Square

The Corn Exchange backs onto the town hall, which is on the site of a couple of old taverns, St Mildred's church, the Corpus Christi Guild Hall and the aforementioned Court of Common Pleas. Condemned prisoners were dragged from the court onto the town square in front, known as Cornhill, to be punished or executed. A thriving market grew up to supply the onlookers with refreshments. One of the people tried there was Alice Driver, who was arrested in 1558 for not attending church. She explained that she preferred the new Protestant methods; an anathema to the majority of Catholics at that time.

Alice's ears were cut off for insulting the Queen and she was tried for heresy. No lawyer would defend her, since heretics were usually found guilty and all property forfeited to the Crown, including their fees. Besides that, to take sides with a heretic was to place oneself under suspicion. So, Alice had to defend herself, which by common consent she did very competently. She argued points of law with the prosecution and quoted vast sections of scripture in response to the accusations of the clerics. Inevitably though she was found guilty and sentenced to be burnt at the stake.

Some commentators on that barbaric form of torturous death talk blithely about the victim being tied to a stake, but the reality of what actually would happen is much more barbaric. They used chains, one around the ankles, another round the waist and the third around the neck. It was rare to record people's last words then, but Alice Driver must have made a big impression on people there on 4 November 1558. As they attached the neck chain, she was defiantly heard to say, 'This is a goodly neckerchief. May God be blessed for it'. Her defiant shade is sometimes sighted lingering in the darker corners of the Cornhill and she is commemorated with eight other Protestant martyrs by a monument in Christchurch Park.

Beside the Town Square stands the Golden Lion Hotel, where a man once murdered his mistress who demanded that he leave his wife. The room still has unexplained temperature drops and on occasion 'something' holds the door firmly shut. A flattened mummified cat was once found in a wall, presumably put there to keep evil spirits away.

Across the road the Debenhams store was once home to the ghost of a woman with a contorted face who roamed around the café scaring off a team of shopfitters. The accounts show how they forfeited the work to another company and had to pay a contract penalty clause for not finishing the job on time!

Above Lloyds Avenue is a collection of offices. A female worker there would, on some mornings, call 'hello' to a cleaner at the end of the corridor. Arriving later one morning she encountered a different cleaner and on describing her usual early morning fellow occupant the cleaner went white and exclaimed, 'That is the woman I replaced. She left here one morning and got knocked down dead outside. She has been dead for two years!' The lady never saw her other cleaner again.

A Habit of Haunting

Between 1130 and 1298 Ipswich had four friaries. Two Austin Canons had places at Holy Trinity Priory and the Priory of St Peter and St Paul. The Carmelite White Friars were situated where the Buttermarket Centre now stands and the huge Dominican Blackfriars complex occupied an area between Foundation Street, Star Lane and the town defensive bank and ditch that ran parallel to Lower Brook Street.

The Black Friars originated in Spain in 1216 and the Ipswich establishment was closed down by Henry VIII's Dissolution of the Monasteries in 1538. The ruins of St Mary's church and their private chapel can still be seen. The complex also originally housed two hospitals (one for lepers) and a library. Inevitably, there is a reputed haunting of a Black Friar on the site, who hovers above the ground (presumably the level has changed) and who points at or, more disturbingly, pokes people.

That last point is worth remembering while noting a tale attributed to Tooley's Almshouses. The almshouses are situated in Foundation Street and were set up in 1551 by wealthy Tudor merchant

The ruins of the Dominican Black Friars' buildings near Foundation Street, Ipswich,

Henry Tooley to provide for some poor widows of the parish. It remains a very pleasant charitable retirement home with an excellent reputation and was largely rebuilt in early Victorian times.

The staff there occasionally see the ghost of a lady sitting and sewing, upstairs in the oldest block. Her appearance usually gives them a couple of days' warning that one of the elderly residents will die. But it is the tale of an early morning visitor that is of greater interest.

A man used to work down the road from the almshouses for EADT newspapers. He walked to work each morning between 4.30 and 5.00 a.m. Since it was his job to drive a van full of newspapers out to the various newsagents, they had to have them early enough to mark up for their delivery boys. One day, after clocking off work at lunchtime he saw an acquaintance digging in the beautiful garden in front of the Tooley's Almshouses. He enquired if one of the residents had passed away, as he had seen the vicar knocking on a door there as he went past. The gardener replied that he couldn't have done, as that particular door hadn't opened all the time he'd been working there. With that they both walked over to the door in question. The hinges were rusted and weeds and cobwebs demonstrated its disuse. It was only then that the man began to wonder just exactly who, or what, the vision in long black flowing clothes, that he had seen so early in the morning, had really been.

It is possible that the apparition he witnessed was the same mysterious character seen at Blackfriars. From a distance, knocking, poking or pointing all look the same. A great deal is known about Blackfriars from the pioneering work of an amateur Ipswich historian called Nina Layard. Wherever they went, they built in the same pattern, which would put the dormitory where the almshouses now stand, not forgetting that the almshouses were started around thirteen years after the Dominican brothers were closed down. The new building may even have used part of the old, or recycled the valuable building stone. What we also know is that their first prayers were at 5.00 a.m., before breakfast. In the days before alarm clocks, it is probable that those cloisters would have

Tooley's Almshouses, Foundation Street, Ipswich – home to two very different ghosts.

needed a knocker-upper. Perhaps this is the identify of the mysterious figure? A resident from the new flats that overlook the ruin has heard beautiful chanting, but is not frightened by it.

The Carmelite White Friars dwelt on a site now occupied by the Buttermarket Shopping Centre. It also covers a large Anglo Saxon burial ground and the remains of some medieval houses, one of which burnt down, judging from the remains. In what had been its cellar, a frail basket was found with half a dozen oval charcoal objects inside. The laboratory found that this was the remains of some sourdough rolls, turned to charcoal by the heat of the blaze and is the only seventeenth-century cooking remains in the whole of England. However, the Buttermarket itself has some less tangible remnants. The closed circuit TV cameras often detect moving shadows when there is nobody else about.

A female attendant from the complex's underground car park went to empty the coin machine at the end of the day, after everyone else had left. She sensed a movement behind her, turned and saw moving shadows. The sighting was checked and confirmed by the video footage and procedures have subsequently been changed, so that in future staff do not have to undertake this creepy task alone.

The Rocking Chair

A husband and wife team of contract cleaners have an interesting story to tell. They were sent to take over a contract in Foundation Street, at a building once used by the architects John, Slater & Howard. It stands opposite Tooley's Almshouses and beside a plot where Gainsborough, the famous artist, once lived. One night, the wife went down to the basement to get some more cleaning materials, but came back upstairs in a hurry. Gasping to her husband, she told of seeing a man in a rocking chair, with a cap on and smoking a pipe. He confirmed that he had seen the ghost too, but didn't want to worry her.

Old Winter

Just off Foundation Street is a multi-storey carpark. It stands on the site of an old network of narrow, terraced streets. It was a very close-knit community that lived there and is believed to be where a character called Old Winter lived, around 1795. He was a cunning man and a wizard in a time when most communities used the services of wizards and witches (or wise women). Most were never written about by the higher classes and were left to dispense love potions, spells and herbal remedies to the poor, so long as they never caused trouble. Old Winter must have made quite an impression though, since three separate written references to his life can be found.

He was walking late at night and saw a man stealing vegetables from a garden. He pointed at him and the miscreant was frozen to the spot all night, unable to move or escape the cold and damp. In the morning others came along and surmised where their missing vegetables had gone. Eventually Old Winter himself came back and gave a wave of his hand and the man was released; he soon made himself scarce.

Another time, a farmer came in need of help. A barn had blown down and he was trying to repair it, but the materials kept going missing. Unable to replace these items as he was so poor, the farmer asked Old Winter for help, who agreed and proposed to hide and keep watch that night. The farmer said he knew a good vantage point and would keep him company. Late at night, a farm worker was seen to step out into the moonlight from the backdoor of his cottage. Crossing the field and stile, he hefted a large beam of seasoned timber onto his shoulder and started to return. By the time the pair had climbed out of their hiding place, the theiving farm worker was halfway across the field. Old Winter pointed his fateful finger at the man, who was suddenly completely confused. He could not find his cottage or the stile and the timber appeared to be stuck to his shoulder and weighed heavier by a second. He stumbled round in a blind panic until Old Winter and the farmer caught him up. Old Winter's hand was waved and the man found the farmer in his face. So once more, the cunning man's reputation grew.

In previous times, the mothers from the area off Foundation Street would threaten their children with the 'bogey man' if they didn't do as they were told or come in for tea. 'Old Winter will get you,' they cried. It is impossible to know if they knew who he was, but it is remarkable that his name lived on for 150 years. That is not the last we shall hear of him either!

Spontaneous Human Combustion

A spontaneous combustion usually occurs to a person who goes up in flames, while not setting light to the area around them. These mysterious occurrences span history and geography. There is a famous set of photographs from Brazil of a woman consumed by fire except for her feet, which often seems to be a common feature. A TV documentary, using time-delayed cameras over a six-hour period filmed the body of a dead pig, which had been clothed and set on fire. The initial flame shot up three feet and if it had been a living person they would have perished from asphyxia or heart attack straight away. After the initial flare up, the flame reduced to a quarter of an inch, spreading all over the clothes. The heat of the flame had sucked fat from the body and the clothes acted as an 'external wick'. Heat burned up more fat, until the whole body was consumed – the clothes were the last to go. Curiously enough, the trotters remained since they are free of most fat, just like human feet.

While this semi-scientific explanation may satisfy some, let us look more specifically at possibly the only instance of spontaneous human combustion heard of in East Anglia. Angel Lane is a small cul-de-sac beside Fore Street Swimming Baths and used to be larger until the road layout changed. A fisherman's wife, sixty-year-old Grace Pett lived there and she had two adult daughters. One had married and moved abroad to Gibraltar. One day, this daughter came back to Ipswich with her husband and a celebration was called for. The mother's husband was out on his boat, but she went for a meal with the couple plus her other daughter, who lived locally. At the end of the night the foreigners went off to an inn to sleep, while Grace and her single daughter returned to a shared bed at Angel Lane.

On the night of 9 April 1744, Mrs Pett did not sleep well. When her husband was away she sometimes came down to smoke a pipe by the embers of the fire, but apparently it was very low that night. Imagine her daughter's horror the next morning when just the ashes of her mother were left and her body still smouldering like a log. Only her booted feet remained. A candle had burnt down to a stub and inflammable items nearby were not affected. At the time the case was credited to her being intoxicated with inflammable liquor spirits, but this was later denied.

It is unlikely that the fire was active enough to spark a cinder, but the woman may have fell asleep with a lit pipe. There was another rumour that a local farmer called Garnham had gone to Old Winter and asked how to destroy her as an enemy. Garnham believed she was a witch and that she had bewitched his sheep. Old Winter refused to do the deed, but said a sheep given her name and burnt alive would achieve the wicked aim. It is alleged that Garnham's wife did this with the aid of a servant and the poor animal nearly escaped when the bandages binding its legs burnt through. However, Mrs Pett died and the facts of her death were recorded by a newspaper reporter visiting the town. It was a young Charles Dickens, who was so influenced by the story he reported that he later copied some of the details into one of his fictional stories – Bleak House.

The Blue Coat Boy

The boy in this story could almost be a character in one of Dickens' novels. His family was poor and his father a dock worker who would return drunk on payday and beat his wife and children. Because most of the family income went on beer, the lad went to one of four poor schools in the town. These were started in the 1700s, supported by churches and the gentry. John Gibbon and John Pemberton started some around 1717/18. The pupils either wore a grey or blue coat to cover their ragged clothes and also identify them as belonging to the school. The schools were in St Matthews Street, Smart Street, Bond Street and Waterworks Street. The lad in question went to the latter, which was rebuilt in the 1800s and is now private housing. The schools gave basic lessons in the three 'Rs' plus plenty of religious instruction and harsh discipline. Some meagre food was provided at midday.

One day in winter, the schoolmaster announced a holiday. While the other pupils may have been glad, our little waif shivered under his coat at the thought of going home. It was payday and his violent father was bound to return drunk. So he came up with a plan to hide himself in the school rather than go home to face another beating. What he did not realise was that the school was due to be closed for two weeks, rather than the couple of days he expected.

The schoolmaster locked up and the boy was left hiding in the dark inside. No light or fire burned, there was no food in the cupboard and even water, which was supplied from a well down the road, was unavailable. His parents did not find him there until the school re-opened, two weeks later. Perhaps they had presumed he had run away. It is certain that his cries for help went unheeded. Weak and undernourished he had succumbed to thirst, starvation and cold, but some say that his pathetic cries for help can sometimes still be heard.

The Poltergeist of Eagle Street

Back in the 1930s a shop in Eagle Street was turned into a café, but plates and cutlery flying around frightened the owners and their daughter so much that they soon sold it on to others who 'didn't believe in that sort of thing'. They soon had to though, when activity increased and plates started to smash against the walls. The second set of owners quit and the place was left empty for a year. No local person would touch it because of its reputation and the stories about it carried in the local press. A couple from London took it on, unaware of the history, and they and their daughter were also plagued by cruet, cutlery and plates being dashed from tables. It has often been thought that physical poltergeist energy seems to be sourced unwittingly from an adolescent on site. An exorcism failed to work and they finally gave up when an empty table and chairs juddered across the room from one wall to the other at around 3.00 p.m., in front of a dozen witnesses. The place stayed empty through the war years and beyond and I remember my parents using the phrase, 'I suppose the ghost of Eagle Street did that' for anything unexplained.

In the 1960s the place was bought and the new owners knocked through into next door to make a larger double-fronted shop. As far as I know, there has been no manifestation since, but businesses rarely last long there and a Dutch student I met who rented a cheap flat above the shop was moving to a dearer alternative 'because it does not feel right.'

Further along the road a grotesque head gazes across at more student accommodation which has a whispering voice on the stairs. Around the corner in Bond St, the ghost of a fireman haunts more student rooms converted from an old fire station. He was finishing a repair job in the yard when a shout went out. His colleague went in his place and died when a wall fell on him. The fireman believed it should have been him and hanged himself two months later.

The Organists

When the Buttermarket was being built, the disused St Stephen's church opposite was used as a site office and contractor's store. Apprentices were frequently nervous about fetching stuff from there alone, no doubt having been influenced by the tales of their work mates. After the completion of the building project, the Ipswich Tourist Information Centre moved into the church, which is when the numerous reliable reports of a pair of ghosts occupying the area where the organ once stood began. Because of that, these spooks became known as 'The Organists'. The pair were ladies, apparently in their sixties, in the ordinary clothes of today. On investigation, two prime candidates for who they had been were identified.

In the latter days of the building's use as a church, the vicar left, as the congregation dwindled to only a handful, a result of the lack of houses left in the parish since the redevelopment of the town centre for more shops. Two ladies, however, were determined that the place would keep going and came in each week to polish pews, arrange flowers and even play the organ when they opened each Sunday. Eventually the church authorities found the upkeep too costly for such a miniscule congregation and closed the church. The ladies were very upset and died in quick succession afterwards.

Several people have recalled them: one lady sold them flowers; while another gentleman said he used to sell them cheap fish, to feed the large number of cats they kept in their house, when he closed up on Saturday nights.

This particular story was confirmed by a lady a couple of years later, who told me that the pair, Ruby and Mimmie Humblestone, were her great aunts and lived at No. 144 Woodbridge Road, Ipswich. She spoke of how strict they were and how they never married but lived together caring for their twin passions; a large number of cats and St Stephen's church.

More Buttermarket Ghosts

The street that actually bears the name Buttermarket is thought to be home to a collection of ghosts of its own. An ex-owner who hanged himself on the top floor haunts the old Limmers Tavern, and Jones' shoe shop, which once occupied the place where Contessa now stands, used to have a haunted cellar. The toilet would flush on its own and the poor old manager used to have to go down in search of shoes, since his two female assistants wouldn't go down alone. Around the corner, in Dial Lane, there is a haunted coffee shop. A bit further along the Buttermarket, one can see the remains of a blocked-off lane running down the side of a building society. It used to go all the way through to Old Cattlemarket, making a slight dogleg bend to the right by the old Cowell's printing works. However, it was at about that point on the lane that some people had their interest diverted elsewhere, by a man running at speed towards the Buttermarket. He was only ever seen by people walking away from the Buttermarket and he appeared running around the bend, coming towards them. Some people stepped aside to make way for this chap, who was obviously in a hurry. Yet, although he passed them, he never reached the exit … but simply disappeared.

The Riddle of Ridleys

Some older readers may remember a splendid department store called Ridleys in Ipswich. A pair of ladies used to run one particular department and had the additional duty of going in early to start up the boiler in the basement. One morning, one had just arrived and heard heavy breathing. Expecting it to be her colleague who had maybe rushed too much, she called out to her. There was no reply and when her friend arrived later, she found the lady in a very distressed state and unwilling to ever enter the basement early again.

Later that morning, she recounted her tale in the staff canteen, sat in her customary place near to the man in charge of the gents' outfitters department who told her very conspiratorially that he believed her. He told how sometimes a Cavalier in full armour would walk across his department in the afternoon when it was quiet; he had never said anything in case it affected his prospects there!

The Ancient House

This imposing building, standing on the corner of Buttermarket and St Stephens Lane deserves its own entry, due to a splendid story that unfolds there. It was built in the late 1500s and after passing through a couple of owners remained in the hands of the Sparrowe family (some of whom are buried in the crypt of the nearby St Lawrence church) for the next few centuries. The building used to contain an excellent bookshop, but it wasn't just those delights that lured people in – for an old sixpence one could enter the secret priest-hole. Sat on a chair was a life-size wax figure of Charles II who was at that time believed to have hidden there after fleeing the Battle of Worcester in 1651 (although historians have since come to believe that he escaped via the South Coast to the Continent). It is quite conceivable that other fleeing Cavaliers may have taken refuge here though and it is highly likely that a Catholic priest may have used this room to hide from the authorities. Ipswich was a staunchly Puritan town during the English Civil Wars, but there were a few Catholic, Royalist supporters, such as the Sparrowe family, who would have been mainly confined under house arrest. Religious persecution was nothing new and a family story about a portrait hanging in the house was that it was of a sixteenth-century ancestor, Gosnall, who was partly responsible for the persecution and execution of nine Protestant martyrs in Ipswich. The family tale concluded that he was eaten alive by rats, although no details survived of how it happened.

If you look on the outside of the building there is some wonderful pargeting (decorative plasterwork). As well as some odd figures of beasts and people, the four front bays depict the four known continents at the time. Australasia is missing, since it had not been discovered by Cook then. In the middle is a large coat of arms, surmounted by the logo 'C II R'. This refers, of course, to the restoration of the monarchy for Charles II and was therefore erected long after the house was built, probably in celebration by the Sparrowe family of 'their' side eventually winning.

The Ancient House, whose pargetting includes depictions of only four continents, since Australia had not been discovered at the time this was designed.

Staff at the Ancient House would often tell stories about the ghost of the Grey Lady who haunted the place.

More than a decade ago, the shop became vacant and was eventually let to Lakeland Plastics. A new manager, who was unfamiliar with Ipswich, was brought in from one of their other stores. He recruited a local staff, who soon told him of the existence of the Grey Lady. He initially thought it was the locals teasing him, until a few unexplained events occurred. Two carefully constructed displays collapsed and one night, when he was working alone, a pair of scissors vanished, only to reappear in another room he had not visited. Disturbed, he called in a spiritualist medium.

She was not from the area and didn't know anything about the house or its history. By the time she visited, the shop had opened and she bumped into the manager just inside the door. Introducing herself she was quick to say that the haunting was genuine: it was female and from a long time ago. Encouraging him to continue with his work, she set off around the premises to see what else she could ascertain. On her return to his office, she admitted that she could do little more than confirm her original impression: the spirit was female, from a long time ago and was unhappy. She had tried to get a name from the spirit, but felt that all the new shop signs saying 'Lakeland' had confused her. She left the shop manager feeling reassured that he wasn't being made a fool of.

A possible origin of the Grey Lady may be found in a connection with Matthew Hopkins, the so-called Witchfinder General. The son of a Great Wenham clergyman, Hopkins had originally worked for an Ipswich shipping firm and practised a little law, but was unsuccessful at it and eventually returned to his home in Mistley, Essex. There is no evidence that he qualified as a lawyer, as is often alleged. He came up with a plan to hunt down witches, starting in Essex and moving

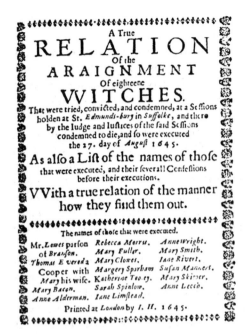

A True
RELATION
Of the
ARAIGNMENT
Of eighteene
WITCHES.

That were tried, convicted, and condemned, at a Seſſions
holden at St. *Edmunds-bury* in *Suffolke*, and there
by the Iudge and Iuſtices of the ſaid Seſſions
condemned to die, and ſo were executed
the 27. day of *Auguſt* 1645.

As alſo a Liſt of the names of thoſe
that were executed, and their ſeverall Confeſſions
before their executions.

VVith a true relation of the manner
how they fiⁿd them out.

The names of thoſe that were executed.

Mr. *Lewes* parſon of *Branſon.*	*Rebecca Morris.*	*Anne Wright.*
	Mary Fuller.	*Mary Smith.*
Thomas E vered a Cooper with *Mary* his wife.	*Mary Clowes.*	*Iane Rivett.*
	Margery Sparham	*Suſan Manners.*
	Katherine Tooty.	*Mary Skiner.*
Mary Bacon.	*Sarah Spinlow.*	*Anne Leech.*
Anne Alderman.	*Iane Limſtead.*	

Printed at *London* by I. H. 1645.

The frontspiece of a pamphlet describing the execution of witches in Bury St Edmunds during the purge by Matthew Hopkins, Witchfinder General and son of a Great Wenham clergyman.

onto Suffolk, Norfolk and Cambridgeshire. In about fourteen months, around 1645, he amassed an estimated £60,000 from charges to councils for ridding their towns of witches. It is true that he had to pay a couple of assistants (including John Stearne and Mary Phillips) and an army of informers, but he was still left with a fortune. For example, he charged Aldeburgh £6 and Stowmarket £23 – enormous sums of money in those days. He was responsible for the deaths of approximately 472 people; over half the total number of executed witches for the UK at that period.

People have sometimes wondered how he got away with it? They may forget that England was in the midst of a Civil War, with magistrates taking on major cases far beyond their usual authority and the population in turmoil. Some even believed that the end of the world would happen soon. It was easy for some poor unpopular widow on parish relief to be accused of being responsible for a hen refusing to lay or a poor harvest. After arrest they may be kept awake for days and nights on end, stripped and examined for 'witch marks' (such as a mole or wart) and pricked constantly to expose it. Small wonder that some signed some bizarre confessions before being hanged. It was the practice to hang witches in England. They were burnt in Scotland or on the Continent, but that death was reserved for those accused of other crimes such as treason in England. It was said that Hopkins was well in with the Parliamentary commanders, who visited him three times. There is the inference that they used his army of paid informers and got rid of suspected Royalist sympathisers or spies for whom they had no evidence via him. In exchange, he was allowed to call himself Witchfinder General and operate without impunity around East Anglia, until a Puritan vicar, John Gaule of Staughton, published a pamphlet denouncing him as a greedy charlatan. Hopkins became ill (possibly from tuberculosis) and was buried in Mistley in 1647.

To return to Hopkins' actions in Ipswich, I found out that according to Ipswich Borough Sessions six people were arrested; one man and five women. The man and four of the women were sent for trial in Bury St Edmunds. James and Mary Emerson were convicted of witchcraft and for sending lice to Mary and Robert Ward. They were sentenced to a year's imprisonment and to four times standing on the pillory. James was found not guilty of the murder of Richard Greye and his wife not guilty of sending lice to John Seeley.

Rose Parker (the wife of Christopher) was found not guilty of witchcraft and the murder of John Cole. She was also found not guilty of felony and feeding imps. Margery Sutton, the wife of James was found guilty of felony and witchcraft. Sureties for good behaviour were required. Alice Denham was found guilty of felony, witchcraft and feeding imps. She was hanged.

But what of the sixth? Her name jumped off the page at me – Widow Mary Lackland. My interest was piqued as to why she was treated differently. She was accused of harbouring three familiars comprising of two dogs and a mole and killing various people with the help of them. Her alleged victims were: her husband John; Sarah Clarke, the servant of Mrs Jennings (with whom she had a small financial dispute); and Elisabeth Aldham. Mary Lackland was also accused of casting away Henry Reade's ship and of murdering him and wasting away the body of John Beales, the tutor of her grandchild. The court record says that Mr Beale was killed after 'he would not have her' after the death of her husband; in other words he rejected her advances.

Inevitably, just as in murder trials today, the court recorded the victim's name, age, occupation and address. You can see for yourself, in the archived document, the name of John Lackland, Mary's husband. He was a barber 'who doth dwell above his business in St Stephens Lane'. Barbers were good middle-class professionals in those days, taking on surgery and dentistry as well as trimming hair. The address, where he lived above the shop is next door to the Ancient House, which sits on the corner of St Stephens Lane and the Buttermarket. So, Widow Mary Lackland was a neighbour of the Royalist Sparrowe family. How close a friend was she and did she visit them? If so, was she suspected of being a Royalist sympathiser or spy?

If she were arrested on trumped-up witchcraft charges, because of a lack of evidence that she was a Royalist, they would not have wanted her to go on trial in Bury St Edmunds. Instead she was tried in Ipswich, found guilty and burnt. The town accounts show a cost of £3 for her execution. Why burnt instead of hanged? The answer to that lies in some obscure seventeenth-century law.

She was alleged to have killed her husband. Her husband was considered a part of the King's authority in each household, so if you killed your husband, you were in effect killing a part of the King. That was considered petty treason, for which the penalty was burning, despite the fact that the people who passed sentence supported a cause that had executed one king and sought to remove all others in favour of a Lord Protector, Oliver Cromwell. If my theory is right, the Grey Lady ghost of the Ancient House is Widow Mary Lackland and the spiritualist medium that thought she had been confused by the 'Lakeland' signs had actually found out her name, despite remaining confused. No wonder she still haunts the Ancient House. She's eager to clear her name and let folk know she was not a witch, but a wrongly accused, close neighbour of this mysterious house.

Feeling Groggy?

The name of grog, given to a mixture of rum and water, was adopted after the Suffolk Admiral Vernon who introduced it onto his ships to combat drunkenness among the sailors, who up until then drank neat rum. The ration was carefully measured out each day. Admiral Vernon's nickname

The Woolpack, Ipswich is home to at least five ghosts, including Admiral Vernon.

of 'Old Grog' came from an old boat cloak he habitually wore, made of a rough silk termed 'grogram' (from the French *gros grain*). It rustled as he paced about the deck. He died in 1757.

He was twice Mayor of Ipswich and captured the Spanish stronghold of Portobello in 1739 with only six ships; a remarkable feat. His home was at Orwell House, beyond Broke Hall in the Nacton area, but he has another 'haunt'.

According to the *Evening Star*, Justin Hum, the chef of the Woolpack Inn on Tuddenham Road, Ipswich was terrified when a ghost scampered through his bedroom. A local medium, Sue Knock, was called and detected the same thing without being told what had happened. She then went on to identify other hauntings in the pub, including a member of the Grey Friar's order and George an ex-landlord who had tried to aid his escape from persecution. The building dates back to the sixteenth-century and has a priest hole.

Most remarkable of all, she identified the fully formed and authoritative figure of Admiral Vernon, as well as the ghost of a Mediterranean-looking sailor. Two of the Woolpack's regulars were taking the mickey out of a sign (affixed with screws to the wall) advertising a ghost tour event, when it fell down and hit one on the head. Old Grog is obviously as accurate with that as he was with cannons.

Andy Johnson, and a team from NCS Paranormal, who measured temperature drops and moving orbs of light in the building and an unexplained flash of light, undertook a separate investigation.

A Drop of Nelson's Blood

In St Clements' churchyard, Ipswich stands a small monument to a man by the name of Sir Thomas Slade, who is buried there with his family. He is remembered for commissioning

The photograph of a child who is said to haunt the Lord Nelson, Ipswich.

HMS *Victory*, the flagship from which that great East Anglian hero, Nelson, fought the Battle of Trafalgar and lost his life. It is appropriate that the church is next to the back of the Lord Nelson pub, the setting of our tale.

The pub dates back to the 1600s and was one of many in the area catering for the needs of the sailors and workers from the nearby dock. A lady held her office party there one January afternoon and at the end of the event the landlord checked to see that everything had been to her liking. All the guests agreed it had been a super meal and that they had enjoyed themselves. The lady, however, had seen a small child at the end of the table, but nobody else could see her! The lady went on to say that she thought it may be a child from a photograph that was on a wall around the corner. They went over and looked and she confirmed it.

The child appears to be three to four years old, in a dress and with dark areas around the eyes. It was thought at the time to be a girl, but it has since been pointed out that boys used to wear such clothes up to the age of five at one time. The picture is one of three found in the loft. One is of a couple, another of a Boy Scout and a girl together with the one of the supposed ghost. From the Scout uniform it has been estimated that the pictures were taken around 1905 and are of the publican at that time and his family. The pictures have since been moved and hang in the lobby leading to the toilets.

Neptune and the Sailor

A pub, similar to the Lord Nelson, stood on the opposite side of Fore Street. It was called the Neptune, but after a period as an antique shop it is now a private house. The owner has said that this pub is haunted and tells of a sailor, or sea captain, who sits on the end of her bed!

The Neptune, Ipswich is home to a typically nautical ghost.

Disasters around the Dock

The main reason for Ipswich's existence and wealth is the ancient port, which enabled goods to be brought from sea up the river Orwell for transport onwards inland, when the roads were poorly maintained and dangerous. The name Ipswich comes from the Old English *Gippeswic* meaning Gippe's port, *Gippe* being a Saxon name. Opposite the Lord Nelson one can see Isaac Lord's, a charming mediaeval merchants' house, warehouse and courtyard. Usually, the gate to the road is closed, but if open it is well worth taking a peep down into the beautiful courtyard. Once in a while, people have done just that, only to jump back and clutch the wall in panic. Thundering up towards them is a horse and cart, careering out of control. There is no waggoner or load and beyond the gate no horse or cart either, because that is where the apparition disappears. It is thought that this is a vivid vision of what is presumed to be a past accident on that site. This ghost appears to be unique, however, since horse ghosts are normally either pulling coaches or ridden by headless riders.

Heading further down the road, past the Neptune and down a narrow alley, a pool hall overlooking the dock can be found. I visited there some time ago, to inspect a particular pool table, which the members said was 'unlucky'. I got a horrid sensation of someone behind me and the manager at that time said that there was often an awful stench focussed around it. They had lifted floorboards in search of dead rats and the like without success.

More recently, a lady who used to work there has described how none of the night staff used to like to clean in that area, since their energy just seemed to drain away and their legs go wobbly. The stereo sometimes switched itself on behind locked doors at night and she also mentioned the ghost of a lady downstairs at the back of the hall in a grey, plain dress, who is seen by staff and customers alike.

At the other end of the docks the old Tolly Cobbold Brewery has its share of knocking, footsteps and mysterious images on the closed circuit TV, but I would like to tell you a tale from nearer to the Old Custom House, which was built in 1844.

When I was in my teens, I would walk through the docks on my way to work, particularly looking out for the distinctive Thames Sailing Barges that were moored by the mills. Often, the workers from Paul's and White Flour Mill would be taking their breakfast outside, since they started loading sacks of flour off the chutes onto lorries by hand very early. It was very dusty and unpopular work carried out by tough, muscular men who nevertheless often succumbed to the dust in their lungs. One chap – the kind who would have been likely to knock any man down who accused him of being fanciful or scared – used to tell the story of Old William.

Once in a while, generally in the early morning, one of the workers would spot a body floating in the dock. The police would be called, but by the time they would have arrived it would usually have disappeared, so divers would be sent into the muddy water and a net trawled through the dock to search for it. With the exception of a couple of dead bodies, which were found, more often than not the results of the search, would be inconclusive. The dockers' folklore attributed these sightings to Old William, a man who had gambled and won a good deal of money at the Green Man public house, which once stood on the docks. Being accused of cheating, he left in a huff and was found a day or so later, floating in the dock without any of his money. Did he stumble in drunk, or was he disposed of after someone had robbed him? We shall never know.

Cranfield's Mill next door to the flour mill provides us with a mystery, unsolved to this day from the time the event happened in the late 1940s. The flour mills were several storeys high (and are about to be demolished as part of the dock redevelopment) and the grain would be elevated to the top, where it would be ground between a heavy pair of millstones. The material would progress down through the building being sieved, checked and sorted into various grades. Between each floor was a pair of trapdoors.

One day it was decided to replace the ten pairs of millstones, as they were getting too smooth and needed redressing or replacing. One of the directors decided he would like a pair to form part of a garden wall, so they were lowered by chains to a waiting vehicle below. The other eight were stacked around the edges of the wall of the upper storey. As it was now knocking-off time, the doors were locked (a safety measure to prevent anyone falling through trapdoors in the dark) and the men went home. It had been a hard day, since the lifting of the giant stones (10ft in diameter and 1ft thick) all had to be done manually with manpower plus block and tackle.

Imagine their amazement the next morning when the doors were unlocked. All the stones lay scattered around the upper storey like tiddlywinks. Someone suggested that it may have been possible (but very difficult) for a couple of pranksters to have entered via the trapdoors, but it was pointed out that you needed a minimum of six men to maneuver one stone. The event still remains a mystery.

From that site one can see the Old Bell Inn by Stoke Bridge. A ghost of a horseman has been seen in the yard there, together with various unexplained 'things that go bump in the night'.

Left: *Isaac Lord's mediaeval merchants' house and warehouse.*

Below: *The Thames Sailing Barge* Centaur. *These wonderful craft can sail in the shallow waters of the East Anglian coast and rivers, since they have movable keel boards mounted on each side of the hull.*

Ipswich Docks including Paul's and Cranfield's Mills and a Thames sailing barge.

The Great White Horse Hotel

This notable coaching inn on Tavern Street can count King George II, King Louis XVIII of France and Charles Dickens among its many notable guests, but it is a 'guest' in Room 305 that is the most interesting. A lady walks through the wall there, allegedly because she died in a fire and the doorway was moved when the room was rebuilt. The event occurred in the early 1920s and the lady's name is thought to be Flossie Fluyd (pronounced Fluid).

Room 209 also has a unique presence. Guests frequently complain about the noisy occupants upstairs disturbing them at two in the morning by dragging heavy furniture around. No matter how frequently the complaints are made and regardless of how helpful the staff are, nothing is ever done… There is no room above Room 209; just a flat roof constructed after the fire.

The Great White Horse, Ipswich, c. 1917. This hotel has played host to two kings and Charles Dickens, as well as some ghosts.

Two Styles of Management

Two offices stand near the corner of Upper Brook Street and Turret Lane. There are strange stories, that tell a tale of contrasting styles of management, relating to both the businesses that once occupied these buildings.

One office manager regularly called in an electrician to attend to an old electric heater. Both he and the electrician knew there wasn't anything wrong with it, but it helped avoid explaining the shimmering haze seen in the corner by some of his more sensitive female staff. Next door the manager was much more honest and told his staff how he had seen the ghost of what appeared to be an old-fashioned nurse on the stairs. The building has subsequently been identified as a 'hospital house' used to provide voluntary care for wounded sailors and soldiers arriving in port during wars against the French. Because of a shortage of hospital beds for ordinary servicemen, the townspeople kindly nursed some in their own homes. Some even took in wounded enemies, who were returned to their homeland if they recovered.

Christchurch Park and Mansion

Ipswich is well blessed with many splendid parks, of which Christchurch Park is the most notable. It was here that Charles II played bowls on his visit to Viscount Hereford and near the entrance the remains of the Holy Trinity Priory can be seen. Part of Ipswich's darker religious history can be seen in the form of a monument to nine Protestant martyrs burnt on the Cornhill

Christchurch Park and Mansion, Ipswich, includes a ghost.

between 1555 and 1558, including Agnes Potter and Joan Trunchenfield, who had assisted their Presbyterian rector, Robert Samuel, who was executed in 1555. Agnes and Joan were executed together on 19 February 1558.

More pleasant is the Christchurch Mansion, which contains a museum and art gallery. The mansion was built in the Elizabethan 'E' form by Edmund Withipoll in 1548 and Queen Elisabeth I visited it twice. The mansion has at least three ghosts; the first of which sounds really charming. It is of a woman in possibly Edwardian dress, dancing around and laughing with the two children whose hands she holds. The various witnesses to her have each independently said that you could not be scared of her – she is so happy.

The second ghost is believed to be a servant girl who died in mysterious circumstances and was investigated by Richard Keeble and Paul Moss-Kemp of the Society for Psychical Research.

The other ghost is also female, but appears in much more ancient garb and has faded to grey. It is possible that this is the same ghost seen at the house (No. 11 St Margaret's Plain) of the motor engineer Mr Stollery, back in the 1950s. A figure in flowing dress would walk from the park side of the living room through to Soane Street. If one was near enough, it is said that the waft of her dress could be felt.

Just opposite St Margaret's Plain and the main park gates, is a triangle of land once used as the Thingstead. This was the Anglo-Saxon court and council; trials by ordeal may well have taken place there. The land contains a later building, the Packhorse Inn. People have seen a red-shirted figure ascending non-existent stairs on its exterior.

Around the corner, on St Margaret's Green, at the Manor House Club a lady ghost, who has startled builders in the ballroom there, has been seen. The property was once owned by the famous Cobbold brewing family and their employee, Margaret Catchpole, later to become the heroine of a local smuggling story, saved their child from drowning in a pond at the back of the house.

The Marvels of McGinty's

The Halberd Inn formed part of the town walls where they turned the corner from Northgate Street across the Tower Ramparts. The old North Gate of Ipswich was demolished long ago, but Archdeacon Pykenham's gateway can be seen nearby. Just like the town gate, it has spikes on top, but the North Gate spikes would have been larger - the heads of particularly reviled criminals were impaled on them. Notice too Oak House with its fine stained-glass windows, panelling and corner-post carving of Wayland, the Saxon god of metal working. What you will not see of course is whatever it is that makes the eerie sounds in the basement and terrifies the staff there.

The Halberd was converted to an Irish theme pub over a decade ago. When they took up the floorboards a functioning well was found, but these actions seem to have stirred up some other, more sinister evidence of the past. On a summer morning, when the coolers and traffic are not making a noise, it is good to rest your head against the deep, cool wall that joins the pub to a

McGinty's, formerly the Halberd, has been the site of an amazing array of strange phenomena.

side alley. You may hear the same sound as many others – the sound of a beating heart, from deep within. It is not known why this should be so.

Harold was the first landlord in the new Irish themed hostelry – McGinty's. One night he closed the pub and gallantly escorted his two barmaids to the taxi office up the road. By the time he returned, his mother-in-law, who had been left alone back at the pub, had barricaded herself into a corner. She was frightened at the sound of feet thumping up and down the stairs behind the open fireplace. Those stairs had been dismantled some years before.

One night, Harold woke at about two in the morning, thinking he could hear noises downstairs. Down he went, all 5ft 2inches of him, armed with a baseball bat. No doors or windows had been forced, but incredibly ten glasses had been smashed in an evenly spaced line on the floor parallel with the bar. Harold searched cupboards and underneath the bar, but couldn't find the culprit. Eventually he returned to bed much puzzled. In the morning, he thought with a clearer head. Hadn't he just had expensive CCTV equipment installed only six weeks ago? Over breakfast, he sat and studied the previous night's tapes. The footage shows the empty bar, dimly lit by the emergency lighting, for twenty seconds then scans other locations around the pub. Upon returning to the bar the video shows two dark shapes on the lit area of the floor – two of the ten smashed glasses. Later, Harold appears in various shots, searching around with his baseball bat. Even if someone could have hidden out of sight of the camera, it is not possible for them to have produced that precise pattern of broken glasses in twenty seconds.

That is not the end of the happenings at this pub. One upper bedroom appears to be haunted and strange sounds are heard, but the pub's exterior is also the location of some strange goings-on. The courtyard had originally been a skittle alley, but in the 1950s there was a craze for air pistols and it was converted into a range. They had experienced problems with this activity as well though. Frequently, a shadow would be seen at the rear of the range near the door. Fearing that someone was inadvertently walking into the firing range, all shooting had to be suspended until the presence was checked out and it was determined that no one was there. After many such incidents the target nearest the door was no longer used.

Around the corner used to be the Tudor Café which experienced poltergeist activity. This stopped, however, after an exorcism was carried out by a local priest.

A Musical Ghost

In sight of McGinty's is the Purple Shop, on the corner of Fonnereau Road. Until recently, Tommo and his wife ran it. Each night they would lock the door and switch off the lights and radio before going upstairs to their flat. In the morning, most unusually, the radio would have already turned itself back on.

Tommo once took his wife out to a meal at Galley's Restaurant in St Nicholas Street. He visited the upstairs toilet. As he reached the top of the stairs, the thumb-latch on the door moved, so he presumed someone was coming out and stood back to let them pass. After a brief wait and no one appearing he entered the small room. There was no one there and no other exit. On leaving, the latch moved again. Finding the manager downstairs he commented on what had happened and was told that he had probably just encountered their 'gentlemanly ghost'. Several of the staff had previously witnessed fleeting glimpses of a male figure up there.

Nearby is the Blackadder pub. Reports relating to the sighting of a ghostly cat, monk and girl have all been made.

Ransome's of Ipswich were famous for their ploughs all over the world, as well as producing the first commercial lawn mower.

That Table

Further up St Nicholas Street, on the opposite side are a couple of properties that have also been the site of certain encounters. There was a wedding dress shop whose owner had experienced trouble when brides came in for their fittings. She had provided a heavily curtained area upstairs for these ladies, who were often accompanied by their mothers, to try on the various dresses and to make alterations as necessary. Some would get the shivers and complained that, 'it didn't feel nice'. Originally the owner thought it might be something to do with them having second thoughts about getting married and that this was a clear-cut case of 'cold feet', but was persuaded that there was more to it. Subseqently, she had the curtain rail moved downstairs and transferred things from downstairs to take its place. But, the foreboding, oppressive feeling remained and was commented upon by many others who visited the shop.

A couple of doors away a new ghost-themed restaurant, called Spooks, opened. It was tailor-made for ghost tours with its gravestone menus and a moving skeleton, but this was not a mere marketing ploy; the owner knew that the place had a haunted reputation. A dwarf was said to have hanged himself from the rafters and his spectre was said to haunt the restaurant. Other apparitions followed. The spectre of a lady, called Sylvia, haunted the downstairs bar, jamming the ladies' loo door and startling customers. Upstairs, in the main restaurant, one table attracted trouble and was known as 'That Table'. If an order was wrong, a drink spilt etc., it was sure to be 'That Table'. One night a waitress took a wooden tray with two drinks on it to a couple seated there. The two drinks, that were set on opposite sides of the tray, simultaneously moved off it and hovered about six inches either side of the tray before crashing to the ground. The frightened couple were excused their bill and the waitress sent home in tears.

A couple of weeks later the same waitress was laying up the tables with a colleague in the early afternoon. "Look at That Table" was the cry. From 10ft away they saw a fork slowly revolve around and around on the tablecloth. The waitress in question refused to work upstairs any more and was given a job behind the bar.

Sacred Earth

Nigel and Anthony have been the proprietors of the Sacred Earth esoteric shop in Upper Orwell Street, for many years. When they first moved in they encountered Edwin, the resident ghost, who they thought was rather exciting. Each night they would call, 'Goodnight' to him and greet him every day with a cheery, 'Good Morning'. They think it is fun to have a friendly ghost on the premises and as they say, it is people that hurt people, not ghosts. Edwin does have one foible though, which is a dislike for pictures hanging straight. Anthony has many diplomas for various skills, such as reflexology and herbcraft, but has given up straightening them on the upstairs wall at the back of the shop, since they were moved so often.

They had always maintained that Edwin spent most of his time in a particular corner of an upstairs room. A new puppy they brought to the shop confirmed this. The dog was carried upstairs and set down to explore. Despite the myriad curious smells and packing materials strewing the floor from a delivery, the dog ignored exploring in favour of waddling straight to 'Edwin's corner' and sat wagging its tail and looking up at a blank space in the corner. It then lay down and slept there; which was to be its practice every day thereafter.

Executions at the County Court

Many people see the castellated roof of the County Hall in St Helen's Street and wonder at its history. Its origins as a court and gaol begin in the 1700s, when public executions were held outside on the triangle of land at the bottom of Orchard St opposite. In those days, before it was ever concreted, birds would not sing there nor would plants grow. The County Hotel was built in such a way that most of the windows were angled to get a good sight of the hanging, drawing and quartering that took place and spectators would hire rooms for a good view. Mary Shemmings of Martlesham was the last woman to be hanged in the gaol [*see* her story under that village's name]. The last execution that took place there, in 1923, was of a farm labourer from East Bergholt who murdered his wife.

The court itself was where Mrs Simpson received the divorce that meant she could marry King Edward VIII. One of the first treadwheels was installed for prisoners there, invented by a Suffolk engineer called Cubitt in 1821.

A chap who worked for the Suffolk County Council there (before they moved to the new site) tells how his colleague was totally sceptical about the paranormal, that is, until the day he went to fetch some photocopy paper. He came out of the room swearing that someone had been 'messing him about' and he wasn't going in there again. Everyone denied playing tricks and he wouldn't say what had happened to him, despite appearing quite shaken. Since he rarely restocked the photocopier anyway, not much notice was taken, except to say the paper was stored in what had been the old condemned cell.

The Furious Father of Freston Tower

Away from Ipswich on the banks of the river Orwell, out towards the Shotley Peninsula, a fine tower can be seen. It was built solely for the education of a gentleman's daughter and each level had a different form of learning attached to it. The top of the tower has fine views across the river and was the obvious choice for the art studio. However, the young lady, cut off from all other social contact, found the view of her art master more appealing and they eloped. Passing sailors have sworn they have heard furious yelling from the spirit of her father in the early evening as they sail by; which was the time her disappearance was discovered.

The Barham Beast

Just outside Ipswich in the village of Barham, an uncanny event took place around 1910. Two men were walking home from work along the main Norwich Road by Barham Church Lane and close to Barham Hall. A large rough-coated dog with big yellow eyes chased them. One of the men tried bravely to beat the beast off with a branch, but the stick passed straight through it. After a while, the dog ran off, straight through a solid brick wall. Was this an instance of the infamous Black Shuck? We shall hear more of him when we visit the eastern side of the county...

Freston Tower, scene of a romantic elopement.

Corpse Way

With an address of Corpse Way, leading to a cemetery in Needham Market ('the homestead of need' in Old English), one could almost predict that a ghost or two would be sighted here. A local man walking there in 1990 saw a lady dressed in blue walking about 50 yards ahead of him. She rounded the bend, disappearing from view. As he turned it too he found she had completely disappeared, with no place to go to. Explaining the strange occurrence to friends later he found he was not the first to have seen her, or to initially take her for a real person. Another man once saw a policeman standing there. Nothing strange about that, except for the fact he was in Victorian uniform and had a look of unearthlyness about him.

The old Waggon and Horses pub in Needham Market was converted into two houses, but it doesn't stop the ghost of an old lady continuing to haunt them both.

Landguard Fort, Felixstowe, where Captain Darell and his men repulsed the last land invasion in England in 1667. The Fort has been considerably altered and added to since then, and was finally abandoned by the military in the 1950s. One can see some of the cranes of Felixstowe Docks looming through the mist in the background.

Landguard Fort

It was at Landguard Point, Felixstowe (on the opposite side of the estuary to Harwich) that a brave Captain Darell and a handful of soldiers fought off the last invasion onto English soil in 1667. Captain De Ruyter (who later became Admiral De Ruyter who commanded the Dutch fleet at the Battle of Sole Bay off Southwold) tried to land some men to pick up food and water. They were returning to Holland having set fire to some of the English fleet in the Thames and Medway rivers. The captain cleverly told his men to lie beneath the ridge of the pebble beach and open fire at it as the Dutch advanced. With each musket ball hitting up to a dozen more pebbles, the Dutch thought that they were outnumbered and retreated.

Landguard Fort was reconstructed to guard against invasion by the French in the early nineteenth century and forms part of a chain of defenses including many Martello Towers along the east and south coasts of England. It is sometimes open to visitors, but a few years ago a person called Jules used to explore some of the outer buildings with a friend called Sally. They sometimes heard eerie, unexplained noises and once went around the back of the fort to see if they could climb a hidden fence. They ran down a set of steps to the fence, but found it impossible to climb. Trying to return, they could not find the steps, as they had disappeared. Thinking back, they had never seen them before on any of their visits. What is more, they never saw them again!

Giving You a Start?

An American serviceman called Billy from the Woodbridge airbase was billeted in old RAF housing at Felixstowe. He describes his experiences like this:

Bawdsey from Felixstowe Ferry. Britain's top-secret radar was developed here.

I was assigned to housing in this complex for probably two months when weird things started happening. The first was small but weird all the same. First let me add that the doors are triple locked, bolt, chain and key lock. Upon awakening to what I thought was a cat moaning, kind of like one sounds when in heat, I went downstairs to get a look-see. I did not notice anything immediately. I looked out of the kitchen door and saw nothing – it is well lighted. I turned towards the back door, when I noticed that the cabinet doors were wide open as well as the drawers. I shut them and continued towards the door. I looked over to my left and my stereo speakers were facing the corners in which they were placed. I then got suspicious and called for my wife to come look. We noticed that the dust surrounding the speakers was undisturbed.

He continued to have odd experiences and once when he asked his wife to shut the door she said, 'Tell the damned ghost to do it'. Joking, he shouted, 'Hey ghost, would you shut that door?' The door shut slowly, by itself.

Three doors down, his neighbour had a job starting the car one morning and asked Billy for his help. After trying everything they were unsuccessful and eventually went in for breakfast. As his friend phoned in to say he would be late, the car outside started up.

Elsewhere in Felixstowe (named after St Felix who Christianised this area), a young girl haunts the railway line where she was killed by a train. You can also get a ferry across to Bawdsey, once top-secret research base for Britain's radar system. The many experimental buildings that detected incoming German aircraft dring the Second World War are now deserted and the gloomy Bawdsey Manor House is now set back beyond the trees. Servicemen would take a quick glance up at the windows as they landed, not just to see if officers were observing them, but also to check if the ghost of a strange former butler could be seen at a particular window.

Decomposed in Clopton

The farmer who owned Clopton Hall until 1928 was a wealthy bachelor, but his single life meant that no-one missed him if he went away for a few days; they simply got on with their work. Eventually, after the farmer had been missing for a prolonged period of time, his decomposed body was found in an outlying ditch and he was given a decent burial. It is believed by some that he has tried to tell them where his money is hidden, as his spectre has reappeared from time to time pulling down bedclothes to attract the attention of past employees and hovering near their beds.

Damned in Debenham

Around a century ago, a lady described Barley House at Debenham. It had a horseshoe (invariably seen as a good luck symbol) nailed onto one of the ceiling beams, purportedly there to trap an evil spirit. She also told of a horse ghost that hung around a pond. A clever vicar tricked it into staying in the pond, by casting a rush light in with it, after having made it promise not to emerge until the rush light burned down – there was little likelihood of that at the bottom of the pond! Rush lights were often just rushes stripped of their outer skin and dipped in animal fat. They burnt with a duller, yellower flame than candles, but were much cheaper.

THREE

EAST SUFFOLK

Letheringham Water Mill

The present mill dates back to 1740, but there has been one on the site since the Domesday Book recorded it in 1070. Back in the 1690s a strange double murder took place there. The miller, John Bullard, and his son were working on accounts, when Jonah Snell, an employee, killed them both with an axe. For some strange reason he then hung their bodies upside down from a beam. He was caught and hanged at Potsford Wood on 14 April 1699, just outside Wickham Market on a green track off the B1078. His body was displayed in an iron-cage gibbet to deter other criminals and the remains of the gallows can be seen there today. Mysterious lights have been seen hovering near the spot, which still feels distinctly uncanny. Snell's victims, however, still occasionally appear to hang upside down in the mill.

In Wickham Market itself, the old White Hart Inn, now converted into an office, claims to be where the ghost of a woman in a sackcloth dress can be seen, while up the road at the Badingham White Horse, someone not of this world walks through the bar. The ghost in Wickham Market is possibly Betty Price; a landlady accused of witchcraft, but the identity of the Badingham spook is unknown.

Bedeviled by Bells

There is a well-documented story of what happened at Great Bealings House, near Woodbridge, during the period from 2 February to the 27 March 1834. Service bells ringing at intermittent intervals plagued Major Edward Moor the owner. The phenomenon was seen and heard by his servants too but despite minute examinations and inspections, a convincing explanation has never been offered.

Spooky Southwold

The old vicarage in Southwold supplies us with the tale of a ghostly woman who apparently kicks up a noise and sits on the four poster bed when people are sleeping in it. Her favourite trick is to make the sound of someone falling down the stairs, but there is nothing to see for anyone who rushes to help.

As you will have read earlier, Admiral de Ruyter commanded the Dutch fleet at the Battle of Sole Bay, off the coast near Southwold on 22 May 1672. The English fleet was commanded by James, Duke of York (later King James II) and the commander of the *Royal James* flagship was Edward Montagu, the Earl of Sandwich. He stayed at Sutherland House in Southwold and met a lovely young serving maid there before putting to sea. So enamoured of her was he that when the Dutch fleet was sighted off the coast, he was the last to put to sea, having dallied with her too long. The smoke from that battle was so intense that it drifted to points off Essex. Both sides claimed a victory and there were huge losses.

Although Montagu joined the battle late, his ship was soon in the thick of the action and sadly he died. But the ghost of his sweetheart still waits for his return at the upstairs window of the Sutherland House tearooms, on the eve of the anniversary of that great sea battle.

The remains of Potsford Gallows near Wickham Market. Jonah Snell, the Letheringham Mill murderer, was hanged here on 14 April 1699.

Southwold Jack strikes his bell in the church. There is a similar figure in Blythburgh.

Above: *Southwold Battery Green – where a celebration led to tragedy.*

Left: *Martlesham Red Lion, scene of the exposure of an infanticide.*

Gun Hill in Southwold has six cannon pointing out towards the area where that battle took place, although they only date to 1745. They used to be fired on special occasions until one exploded, killing a young soldier who is said to still haunt the place.

The cannon were likely to have been preceded by other waterborne warriors long before this. Southwold was named in Old Norse from the Danes who settled there. Its original name of *Sudwold* means south wood.

Murder in Martlesham

A figurehead of a red lion, that was lost in the carnage of the Battle of Sole Bay, was washed ashore and found itself decorating a pub in Martlesham to which it gives its name. That pub, dating back to at least 1711 itself, is haunted by mysterious sounds and knockings, as well as candles flickering or snuffing out for no apparent reason. Maybe it is the ghost of fifty-one-year-old Mary Shemmings who killed her grandchild by poisoning him in 1844. The baby John was exhumed from Waldringfield Meeting House graveyard and brought for examination at a room in the pub, where the inquest was later heard. Evidence was given as to how she objected to bringing up the two unsupported children of her twenty-one-year-old daughter, Caroline, and of her obtaining arsenic. She was hanged in Ipswich by the executioner, Calcraft, before an estimated crowd of 10,000.

Alternatively, the presence at the Red Lion could be the ghost of an airman, probably from the nearby Martlesham Airfield, who has sometimes been seen. Originally the No. 1 Testing Station for the Royal Flying Corps, during the Second World War, the airfield was also used by both the British 264 Fighter Squadron of Boulton Paul Defiants and the American 356th Squadron who lost seventy-two airmen, mainly in Republic P47s and Mustang P51s. The station was also home to the Schneider trophy World Speed Races winner Fl. Lt Sidney Webster in 1927.

Occupants of the Suffolk Police HQ, subsequently built on the site, have seen a similar ghost in the canteen. An additional sentry ghost has been spotted in Portal Avenue (where some dogs refuse to go) and one more by the BT Research Station Gatehouse. There has even been a sighting of a female WAAF.

The *Ipswich Journal* of 24 November 1821 offered a £15 reward for the capture of whoever robbed a grave in St Mary's, Martlesham, churchyard of the fresh corpse of the wife of Capt. Forman of Woodbridge. It seems that bodysnatchers were at large, possibly because of the lucrative trade in corpses to be used in medical dissection. As you will see though, this disturbance of graves did not cease here.

The Deceased of Dobbs Lane

Still in Martlesham, a lonely grave can be seen on the corner of the heath in Dobbs Lane. It marks the spot where a shepherd by that name is buried. He committed suicide in 1722 when his young wife died in childbirth. In 1940, an airman tried to dig at the spot for a prank and ended up running all the way back to his barracks, a very frightened man. He told the astonished guards that he had been chased away by an angry ghost of a young man.

Grave of the shepherd at Dobbs Lane, Kesgrave.

George Carlow's Dole and the Melton Cat

At the rear of the Bull Hotel Woodbridge is a gravestone, despite there being a perfectly acceptable churchyard opposite. It is the last resting place of a horse ostler called George Carlow, who once owned the place. He was a non-conformist by religion and therefore did not want burial at the church. The faded inscription reads

> Here lieth ye body of George Carlow who departed this life the 24th day of March, 1738, aged 76 years.
> Weep for me dear friends no more
> Because I am gone, a little before
> But by a life of piety prepare yourselves to follow me.
> Good friends for Jesus' sake forbear
> To move the dust entombed here.
> Blessed be the man that spares these stones.
> Cursed be he that removes my bones.

> 20 shillings worth of bread is to be given on this stone to the poor of this town on the 2nd day of February forever.

The custom is kept up on a yearly basis, with the tenants of the property taking responsibility for the bread (often now cakes) provision along with the rent. It is said that Carlow will come back to haunt anyone who fails in that duty. He would no doubt have sympathy for Thomas Seckford, an officer at the court of Elizabeth I who died in 1587. He endowed several Woodbridge buildings, including almshouses and reappears in full costume to remind folk to keep his charity going.

There is a similar custom at Bury St Edmunds, where the Cakes and Ale ceremony commemorates a benefactor called Jankyn Smith who died on 28 June 1481. The oldest endowed sermon in the country is preached at St Mary's church and the almshouse residents who attend each receive 'one shilling' (or the equivalent modern amount) before the trustees of Jankyn Smith's charity go to the Guildhall for cakes and ale. It all takes place on the Thursday nearest the date of his death.

At nearby Melton, the Horse and Groom pub has noted the presence of a white lady ghost and a spectral cat that suffocates people in Room 3 by lying on their throats in the middle of the night.

A ghost of a nurse has also been seen at the site of St Audreys Hospital, Melton and was once photographed looking through a doorway.

Spirits From Behind The Bar

Back in 1995 an Essex medium called John Cochrane spent some time at the King's Head, Woodbridge, investigating its more ethereal customers, which he reported in the now defunct *Ghost Hauntings* magazine.

Woodbridge Tide Mill and harbour.

He told of the spirit of a man who had been attacked in 1823 by some criminal accomplices. He gave their names as Brady, Lynch and Tom Boy. A very pleasant young woman of around twenty-two also was visible, in a long dress, pinafore and skull cap and she was joined by a skipping boy. Finally, Cochrane saw some red-coated soldiers come through the wall (where there was once a door), who were probably an echo of the time when Woodbridge was a garrison town in the 1800s.

Burials at Sutton Hoo

Just outside Woodbridge lies the royal burial ground of the Wuffings dynasty. Many people visit it as one of the most important Anglo Saxon archeological sites in Europe. Fourteen burial mounds exist, including the fabulous ship burial excavated by Basil Brown for the owner of the land Mrs Pretty in 1939. What is not appreciated by many is that Mrs Pretty was a spiritualist who saw ghosts on the site. If she had not, she would have never paid for the private excavation that led to the discovery of the most remarkable treasure hoard ever found in the UK. Magnanimously, she donated the priceless treasures to the British Museum, including a helmet, purse with coins, sword, sceptre whetstone, lyre, cauldron and drinking horn and so on.

For many years there was a puzzle about some 'sand men' found in awkward positions

Above: *Reconstruction of an Anglo Saxon helmet from Sutton Hoo. It was most likely a ceremonial piece worn by King Raedwald who was buried in a ship there around AD 625.*

Right: *The mysterious 'sand men' from Sutton Hoo. The bodies dissolve because of the acidic soil, so archaeologists have to rapidly take a cast of the stain in the soil before it dries out and disappears.*

has also been the site of a phantom coach and there is an immovable bloodstain indelibly marked on the floor.

Later occupants of the Hall, before it was demolished, included the Fitzgerald family. Edward Fitzgerald (1809-83) wrote a translation of the *Rubáiyát of Omar Khayyám* and is buried in the local churchyard.

Fear in Framlingham

The Framlingham Crown and Anchor is a pleasant hostelry, albiet with a couple of uninvited extra guests. A mischievous ghost child mixes among the drinkers and is heard, rather than seen, by those sensitive to such things. He talked to medium Sue Knock about a blacksmith and a fatal horse-riding accident and apparently he 'moved' to the Crown and Anchor after being cast out by an exorcist from a house opposite.

It is hardly surprising that the local castle is haunted. The former great hall ended up being used as a poor house at one stage and one of the old occupants still hangs around. It is the castle where Mary I waited and gathered her forces to take the throne of England in 1553 while others were trying to put Lady Jane Grey on the throne. She had been given Framlingham Castle by her brother Edward VI, but it had originally been built and expanded by five generations of the Bigods, who gained the land from Henry I.

Nearby Bruisyard Hall is haunted by a nun and has other uncanny happenings associated with it.

Black Shuck and the Wild Hunt

Black Shuck is the legendary devil dog that roams from Maldon in Essex all around the East Anglian coastline up to York, where he is known as the 'barghuest'. He is also nown as: Padfoot; Galleytrot; Hateful Thing; Old Shug and a number of other regional variants. He has been seen at Barnby, near Beccles; at the bridge over the Hundred Stream, by the river at Geldeston and he has raced through the ruins of Dunwich, that once proud coastal town that has mainly been reclaimed by the sea. (A popular but unlikely story is that the bells can still be heard ringing under the waves.) A coachman hit out at the canine apparition near Reydon, Southwold, but his whip went clean through it. An American serviceman and his wife witnessed it throwing itself against the wooden walls of their hut during a storm one night at Walberswick Marsh. In 1938, an Aldeburgh man encountered it near Ditchingham railway station.

My own favourite tale is of an old chap who used to frequent the Butley Oyster pub. He was walking with his bike up the hill when a huge, shaggy black dog with fiery red eyes came towards him. Thinking he should just keep going, he was amazed and startled when the dog walked straight through him. I hasten to add he was on his way to the pub, not coming from it. This happened in the 1970s. Just as well he did not look into those evil eyes, since to do so means death.

You can still see the scorch mark on the door where Black Schuck tried to claw his way out of the beautiful Holy Trinity church at Blythburgh on 14 August 1577, having killed a man and a boy. The hound has been spotted there on the A12 and more recently between 1978 and 1985 by a policeman called Craig Jenkins. There was also a sighting at Oulton Broad.

Bungay Castle, home of Earl Bigod. A long ballad has the chorus: 'If I were in my castle of Bungay, Upon the river of Waveny, I would not care for the King of Cockney'. After a siege Earl Bigod eventually paid his taxes to the King.

During that same wild and stormy day in 1577 he also visited St Mary's church, Bungay, where two more people were killed. His presence at other sites has also presaged death and destruction. It is thought that Sir Arthur Conan Doyle got the idea for T*he Hound of the Baskervilles* after hearing tales of the beast during a stay in East Anglia.

There have been theories about the beast being one of the Norse god Odin's hounds. The sagas contradict that in saying he had two wolves: Freki and Geri (Greedyguts and Gobbler). However, the Norse god Odin or his Saxon counterpart Wotan are connected with the Wild Hunt, or Furious Host, of spectral hounds that seek lost souls on the gales of winter nights.

Diabolical Bungay

It isn't just Black Shuck you have to watch out for in Bungay. The Three Tuns pub is very haunted. One investigator in 1969 registered twenty-four different ghosts, including a highwayman called Tom Hardy and Rex Bacon, who hanged himself at the top of the stairs there in 1682.

If you really want trouble though try walking seven times around the Druid Stone in the churchyard of St Mary's Priory … this, apparently, will summon the Devil! There is a similar belief about a stone at St Peter's church, Westleton. I take no responsibility for what happens if you try it! Greyfriar's Priory is also noted to be where ghostly footsteps can be heard as well.

Earl Hugh Bigod was a bit of a 'devil' himself in his day and it is said that he had a reputation, along with his family, of being a robber baron. He defied the King in not paying his taxes, but

Gamekeepers. Guns, booby traps and mantraps faced the intrepid bands trying to hunt for what had historically been theirs by right until the aristocracy enclosed land. There are some popular traditional Suffolk poaching songs. One starts: 'I had a long legged lurcher dog, I kept her in my keeping. / She'd run a hare of a moonlit night, when gamekeepers lie sleeping.

an ancient song details how his castle at Bungay was laid siege to and he had to throw whole sacks of gold over the wall to make the besieging army go away.

Finally, Lion's Grave is a spot on the Ditchingham Road out of Bungay, with a maniacal coach and four thundering into the path of unwary motorists.

Baffled in Barsham

The distinctive round-towered church of Holy Trinity lies in the village of Barsham, midway between Bungay and Beccles. Many investigators have been baffled by the phantom footsteps heard in the chancel and have accredited them to the Suckling family, who were associated with the village from the fifteenth century until 1960. A lady in Georgian dress is also seen in this area and lights unexplainably switch on and off.

The churchyard too has its ghosts. One is reckoned to be the wraith of Old Lady Itchingham who died in 1584 at the incredible age of 110. The other ghost is much more modern and is believed to be of the writer Adrian Bell who died in 1980. Several other ghosts have been seen here in mediaeval dress and the nearby plague pit is suspected as their source. The rectory itself doesn't escape paranormal activity. Objects move around of their own accord and in a room, where a priest hole is concealed, lights are seen and footsteps heard.

Worried in Walberswick

You will rarely find such as exact time for a haunting as this one: a man called Eric Blair was sat outside of the church in Walberswick on 22 July 1931, at around 5.20 p.m. He was sketching, when he saw a small stooping man enter the churchyard. Hoping he would be able to gain access inside (the church was locked) Eric followed him, but the figure vanished. The figure had no other exit to use to get out of the church and, in fact, Eric found that the door he had entered through was still locked. He noted the event in his diary and discussed it with local people, who confirmed that the figure he had seen, dressed in brown, was a locally known ghost. Eric Blair, who took up the pseudonym George Orwell, later became more famous for writing the books *1984* and *Animal Farm*.

There is another locally well-known tale. Visitors using the ferry have urged the boatman to wait for a couple they have seen hurrying towards it, but he ignores the pleas, as he knows they will never arrive. They drowned in an accident many years ago.

Blytheswood Lodge (sometimes also known as Westwood Lodge) is the site where the ghost of a woman is said to haunt. She wears a silky kind of dress and a local gamekeeper, not known for his temerity, has refused to work around the area having frequently seen her there. Three policemen who kept a vigil one night have backed up his claims.

The Haunting of Black Toby

There is a picnic site just off the A12 near Blythburgh called Toby's Walks. According to entries in the *Ipswich Journal* of 1745, it is named after a black soldier, Tobias Gill, who was stationed locally with Sir Robert Rich's 4th Dragoons. On the evening of 26 June 1750 Tobias walked drunkenly across the heath and the next day a Walberswick girl, Ann Blakemore, was found dead there. The villagers (hostile to the troops quelling smuggling) deduced that he was responsible, since he was found in a drunken stupor nearby. Despite his pleas of innocence, a death sentence

An octogenarian musician, who used to tour the Leiston area with his wind-up musical box.

was passed at Bury on 25 August that same year. He was sent back to the Walks to be hung and while still protesting his innocence he begged for the noose to be tied to a moving mail coach (instead of the tree) so that he could run for his life. The request was refused. After his execution at Blythburgh on 14 September people asked questions and it came to light that no marks had been found on the young girl's body and her clothing was not disarranged. People started to have second thoughts, but it was too late and his corpse was hanged in chains.

The girl came from an outlying farm and rarely came into the village, so would have probably been unaware of the black man's presence; a rare sight in those days. Might she have encountered him walking out of the mist and thought him the devil? A heart attack might then have been the cause of her death, but Black Toby still patrols the area to remind people of their injustice.

The pub that Tobias Gill had been drinking at beforehand was the White Hart and this was used as an ecclesiastical courthouse in the thirteenth century. A knocking was heard from an old oak door, but there appeared to be nobody there, not even the monkish figure that appeared elsewhere. To my knowledge there have been no more reports since a serious fire in 1967.

Blythburgh was once much more important than today, with a gaol and mint and two annual fairs. Gilded angels line the roof of the enormous Church of the Holy Trinity and a bell – very similar to 'Southwold Jack' – striking a wooden soldier once regulated the time. Black Shuck once entered here and scorched his mark on the north door.

Not far away is the Blyford Queen's Head where some mysterious sounds, plus small luminous balls of light, several of which were pursued through walls by a party of people in 1969, have been heard.

Saxmundham, Leiston and Blaxhall

Saxmundham has a very well turned-out ghost. A man walked down the High Street, heading towards the fish and chip shop for his supper. Walking towards him on the opposite side was a ghost in top hat and tails. He took him for someone in fancy dress at first before realising he was not of this world. In the fish shop, other customers told him he wasn't the first to spot their high-class ghost.

Down the road in Leiston, the White Horse Inn was subject to severe poltergeist activity. Moving glasses, opening and closing doors and bottles throwing themselves off shelves were all experienced, until an exorcism took place.

Maybe the White Horse should borrow the 'Growing Stone' of Blaxhall to weight its moveable objects down. The object on Stone Farm is said only to have been the size of a small loaf of bread a century ago, but is now estimated to weigh 5 tons.

Harmful Halesworth

You may be familiar with the nursery rhyme *Goosey Goosey Gander* in which an old man who wouldn't say his prayers is 'taken by the left leg and thrown down the stairs'. It is believed to refer to Puritan attacks on Catholic priests.

Chediston Street in Halesworth is sometimes known as 'Cherry Bow' and was a location for several taverns and their associated small breweries. The ghost of Squire Baker is reputed to haunt this street. He must have liked that rhyme, because he is renowned for throwing the vicar down the stairs, breaking his legs.

There is also a heavy-footed ghost that walks into a house and clumps noisily through to the other side. Maybe it is connected with the brutal murder of policeman PC Ebenezer Tye in 1862. John Ducker was convicted of the deed and was the last person to be publicly hanged in Suffolk in 1863.

The Merman of Orford

Orford Castle started to be built in 1165 by Henry II and helped him to maintain authority against the revolt of 1173-74, which inevitably included Earl Hugh Bigod who up until that time had Bungay, Framlingham, Walton (now beneath the sea off Felixstowe) and Thetford castles as well as claims on Norwich. Orford Castle was built at a very strategic point, overlooking the sea to prevent incoming reinforcements and also commanding a ford across the river. Orford's Old English name includes the word *ōra*, which denotes a shore as well as the ending of ford.

More than a century later a celebrated event took place there within Suffolk folklore, written about by the chronicler Ralph of Coggeshall. Some fishermen caught a wild, naked man in their nets, who had to be restrained in order to keep him in the boat. He had very long hair and a beard. He was taken to the custodian of the castle, who confined him to a cell while deciding his fate. The 'merman' as he came to be known did not speak and would only accept raw fish to eat. Many visitors came to see him and the gaolers no doubt earned themselves some tips.

The custodian decided it was cruel to keep him captive all the time so arranged for a cage of nets to be suspended in the water so he could swim. The man looked very pleased at his return to the water and swam around. Then he waved to his captors on the shore and dived deep below the nets. He reappeared on the open-sea side of the barrier, waved once more and was gone.

More recently a visitor took a photograph on the stairs of the keep which seems to show the face of a man peering up at her.

Orford Castle, the temporary home of a merman.

From the top of the castle keep you can see the great shifting shingle spit that forms Orford Ness. It has been created by material washed southwards from the north around the coast. A great deal of coast has been lost through erosion by the sea in Suffolk. Not only was most of Dunwich and Slaughden washed away, but you can witness the sandy cliffs falling into the sea at places such as Pakefield and Covehithe.

At the time of writing, fresh erosion of the Pakefield cliffs has exposed thirty-two flint tools dated to 700,000 years ago. This is very significant because it is the earliest evidence of human activity in the whole of Northern Europe. Until now researchers believed that humans did not cross the land bridge from mainland Europe to the UK until 200,000 years later.

Dunwich was originally an important East Anglian port (as evidenced by the *wic(h)* Anglo-Saxon name ending for a port town). An eighth-century record shows it as *Domnoc*, referring to a Celtic term for a 'deepwater place'. The first Bishopric of the area was established here and later moved to Elmham, as the town gradually sank into the sea.

The Kessingland Monster

The merman is not the only strange creature to be seen in the sea around Kessingland. In the early 1900s, the writer Lilias Rider Haggard excitedly summoned her father Sir Henry Rider Haggard (the author of *King Solomon's Mines* and *She*) from Bungay to their Kessingland summer home. She and her friends had spotted a monster serpent, to rival the one in Loch Ness, just off the coast. It has been reported again since then by people who have maintained they did not know the original story.

The Pipers of Beccles

There is something about rats that make many people shudder. The town folk of Beccles were at their wit's end when a plague of them invaded every house one summer long ago. Not only did they spoil the food, but also it was even then suspected that they carried a devastating plague.

None of the usual remedies for ridding themsleves of rats seemed to work and the peddler, Sam Partridge, saw a chance to make some big improvements to his finances. He enlisted the help of two friends, Peter Harris and Jonathan Betts, a candle-maker. Together they visited a trio of witches that lived together by the river. Fanny Barton, Nancy Driver and Sally Price had an awesome reputation, but people did not tend to visit them unless they were in desperate need of help. They were said to strike a very hard bargain for their services.

No one knows what deal was struck that day with the witches, but we do know what was agreed between the town council and the three men. A sum of 45,000 marks would be paid if they could rid the town of its infestation. Some councillors thought it far too high a price, but others noted that there was little else that could be done. They would not get paid unless they did the job and the town would have faced ruin if the situation persisited much longer.

Consequently next morning, the three men were seen and piping tunes from a set of three bewitched whistles were heard. The inquisitive rats came out from the houses and followed them in an ever increasing procession out of the town. Some said that they were led into the river Waveney and drowned. The town was jubilant and unlike the more miserly inhabitants of

A horseman had the top job on the farm, and often used 'horse whisperer magic' in Suffolk to control his horses. The 'horseman's grip and word' were passed on by secretive societies.

Hamelin in Germany, prepared three bags, each containing 15,000 marks for the three heroes. The money stayed on the table of the Portreeve for some time, guarded by a couple of soldiers, but the claimants never came to collect their booty. (The town had a Portreeve rather than a Mayor from 1584-1835, due to a rather complex and colourful history.) It was suspected that the witches may have known what had happened, but nobody volunteered to go and ask them. People have a fair idea though, as the ghosts of three pipers appear by the river Waveney on 31 August each year.

The Beasts of Beccles

The town name hasn't changed much since its entry in the Domesday Book when it was known as *Becles* from the Old English *bέce* meaning stream or beck and *lές* meaning meadow or pasture land. The town's river Waveney, into which the rats jumped, forms part of the Norfolk border and visitors driving near to it will still recognise the way the town got its name. Originally the sea reached as far as the town, making it an important inland port.

It wasn't a rat but something much larger and more surprising that a Beccles farmer claims to have shot in 1991. He insists that both the police and government asked him to destroy the body of the beast and not tell anyone it was a lynx.

The Crown Inn has a ghost that can be heard going upstairs. It also seems to knock pictures off the wall, so maybe they are not to its taste. A large white dog was seen by a woman walking in the nearby cemetery, which faded as she approached. It is the wrong colour for Black Shuck, so maybe it is the faithful pet of one of the grave's occupants.

Author Pete Jennings, with blackened face during the Old Glory Molly procession, bearing the Cutty Wren at Middleton on Boxing Day.

The Tudor Roos Hall (dating to 1583) on the Barsham Road has attracted a lot of attention over the years from psychic investigators. A coach pulled by headless horses is said to drive up to the front door on Christmas Eve. A colourful addition to the legend is that a beautiful woman alights, but looking into her eyes will bring death or madness. Other sources reckon it contains a member of the Blennerhassett family who once owned the hall and who travel between there and their other home in Norwich.

An oak tree that was once used as a gallows is not only haunted, but is said to be a way of summoning the devil if you walk around it six times. The ghost is of a man hung for stealing, but found to be innocent after his death. He wears an old mottled-brown jacket and torn trousers.

A young lad saw the ghost of a tall woman in a white dress at Jay's Hill, Hulver Street, near Beccles. She faded as he approached on his bicycle. He summoned his family, who felt uncomfortable in the place, particularly when a moaning noise was heard. Since then a motorist has also reported seeing the ghost, who is believed to be a woman from nearby Sotterly Hall who was murdered there by her lover some years ago.

The Cutty Wren

On Boxing Day night in the small village of Middleton, near Leiston, a sinister, sombre procession of people with blackened faces can be seen lit by flaming torches processing to the

Slaughden hamlet was washed away from Aldeburgh. The Three Mariners was a smugglers' haunt.

Aldeburgh Moot Hall. Inshore fishing is important here and so too is their lifeboat, of which they are justifiably proud.

Covehithe church, built within the ruins of a larger one destroyed in the Civil War. It was haunt of smugglers and is the location where a white lady ghost has been seen.

sound of a single drum beat. This is not a supernatural occurence, but rather the Old Glory Molly Dancers and Musicians, carrying out the revival of the Cutty Wren traditional custom, which was recorded there in the early 1900s. The Wren Bearer carries the garlanded pole containing a carving of a wren, which in the old days was a live bird, caught and killed for the procession – part of the dark magic of midwinter.

A large crowd gather outside the Bell Inn to witness the East Anglian traditional molly dances, hear his songs and the story of how the Celts revered the wren as the King of the Birds despite its diminutive size. ('Cutty' means small.) It is a custom known in Ireland, Scotland and Wales, but this is the only place in England with such a recorded history.

Molly Dancing is a particularly East Anglian form of ritual dance, different to Morris and performed in winter. The actions are jerkier and a Lord and Lady lead the disguised dancers. The 'lady' is a man dressed up as a woman. Old Glory features all male dancers and an all female band of musicians. Apart from their blackened faces they have clothes associated with the Suffolk farm workers of a century ago and wear bows of green and black ribbons. Their fierce and serious faces belie the great fun they have in keeping this unique tradition alive.

The Phantoms at the Opera?

Aldeburgh, the seaside town named after an old fort (Old English *Aldeburc*), is famous for its Britten-Pears classical music festival and seafront moot hall. It shares the world-famous concert series with the beautifully reconstructed Snape Maltings nearby. Once, it was the scene of an even more spectacular entertainment, with a battle of phantoms in the sky. These phantoms were watched by the townsfolk on 4 August 1642, between 5.00 and 6.00 p.m. At the culmination of the 'battle' a large stone fell from the sky, though where it landed is not known. If it had been found it may have added fuel to the theory that what had been witnessed was a meteor storm, rather than a spectral one.

Alternatively this sighting could be linked with events in 1916 when a girl claimed to have seen a disk in the sky carrying men dressed like sailors. She said it flew overhead as low as 30ft for around five minutes.

Save us from the Smugglers!

A new parson of Pakefield preached against the lawlessness of local smugglers and was foolish enough to go down to the beach while they were landing goods. They buried him up to his neck in sand and told him if he didn't shut up they'd let him catch the tide.

People imagine smuggling as a couple of chaps with a cask of brandy in a rowing boat. On this coast it was a well-organised, extensive business. As many as 200 men and 100 horses may be involved in runs ashore at places such as Pakefield, Covehithe and Syzewell Gap where the Hadleigh Gang heavily outnumbered the few excise men. They used the sails of the many Suffolk windmills as a coded communications link across the countryside. The Three Mariners inn at the now washed away Slaughden hamlet by Aldeburgh was sometimes used as a rendezvous, with coded chalk marks on the beams letting those 'in the know' when they would be next required.

Along the small cliffs of Pakefield, a wild haired, crazed female ghost can be seen wringing her hands and peering desperately out to sea. She is known as Crazy Mary, a lovely local lass who fell in love with a sailor. He went to sea, never to return … she waits for him still.

> Those roaring boys of Pakefield
> Oh how they did thrive.
> They only had one parson
> And him they buried alive!

So goes a ditty relating to the beach that Crazy Mary overlooks.

Captain Blood and the Oulton Broad Wherry

On 24 June 1851 at 12.30 a.m., a graceful Norfolk wherry called the *Mayfly* sailed on Oulton Broad under the command of the appropriately nicknamed Captain 'Blood' Stephenson. Not only did it have a precious cargo of a casket containing thousands of pounds in gold, but also aboard was his master's daughter Millicent Dormer. The vessel was bound to sail from Beccles to Great Yarmouth.

Blood Stephenson had an evil plan to kill the crew and escape with the bullion out to sea and on to Holland, as well as forcing Millicent to go with him. He killed the mate and dumped him overboard, but the plucky Millicent intervened and he struggled with her. In the ensuing desperate defense, she stabbed him with a knife, but was also fatally injured herself. The cabin boy Bert could not manage the wherry alone and got into a lifeboat. He drifted at sea for some time, but was fortunately rescued and told what had happened. The ship was found drifting with the two corpses aboard and was frequently seen in ghostly form every 24 July. To prevent this, a model wherry is burnt each year at Oulton Broad on August Bank Holiday Monday.

The cabin boy Bert was befriended by Mr Dormer and they first saw the ghost wherry three years after the event while fishing together at Oulton Broad. The elderly Mr Dormer had a heart attack on the spot and died.

A Duel Murder?

More murder and mayhem happened at Oulton House when the owner returned to find his wife in bed with another man. He challenged the lover to a duel with his sword, but lost and was killed himself. The killer left with the errant wife, leaving her daughter behind. As she grew older, she fell for a local farmer, but before she could marry him a veiled woman arrived in a coach at the hall and the girl was found dead. It is thought that the coach contained the returning mother, who was somehow trying to disguise the details of the past, but why or how remains a mystery, as does the phantom carriage and horses that can occasionally be seen arriving at Oulton House.

For a long time only one wherry remained on the Broads, but a couple more have now been restored. This is therefore a rare photo of two racing back in the 1950s.

Look out in Lowestoft

A grey lady haunts the cellar of No. 36, High Street and she is but one of a number of hauntings in the town. At No. 55 a builder was startled in 1974 by a ghostly lady in a long dress and mob cap who climbed the stairs to the first floor. Later that afternoon the owner saw her continue up to the second floor. Maybe she didn't like the dust and disturbance of the building work below.

At the Royal Falcon Hotel the landlord was recently in the news when he requested insurance cover against poltergeist activity, when a mischievous spirit started smashing glasses and moving furniture. I understand that he was unsuccesful.

The site of St Bartholomew's Priory in Mariners Score has ghostly monk figures in attendance and they also seem to like the Anchor Hotel. The Mariners inn also has a haunted basement.

Not all ghosts in Lowestoft are so serious though. Young ladies allegedly have their bottoms pinched by a ghost named George in the toilet of the Sergeant Pepper's Diner.

'What do we do with a drunken sailor?' might be a jaunty nautical ditty, but try telling that to witnesses of the ghost of the Town Bridge, who is said to be that of a drunken sailor who tried to impress his lady love by walking the handrail. He fell in and drowned.

More frightening is the North Quay ghost of Edward Rollahide. He died in 1921, after a fall in which another worker, George Turner, was involved. They had argued during a card game and Edward had chased Turner wielding an axe. However, the assailant's wild attack ended with him falling into a pit of wet cement. The body was never recovered, but the ghost has been encountered several times. One of those appearances was to his old adversary, George Turner, who was so frightened he took to his bed and died.

CURING YARDS, LOWESTOFT

Lowestoft Fisher Lassies. Scots girls came down too by train to process the herring on the quayside. The fishing fleet once numbered hundreds of smacks, but has sadly declined to a handful. The chorus of a local fishing song goes: 'Do you open the pane and pop out the flame, just to see how the wind do blow'. The phrase 'do you' is an instruction rather than a question in the Suffolk dialect, so the chorus tells you to open the window and hold out a candle to find the direction of the wind. The verses go on to detail how each direction of the wind is no good for fishing, which is probably true, since the trade is cold, wet, dangerous, hard and poorly paid.

There is a rather charming animal ghost seen at Grange Farm, Henstead outside Lowestoft. Tommy the horse has been seen on misty evenings grazing alongside another horse that was once his stable mate. Despite dying years ago he still seems to enjoy frolicking in that meadow.

Troublesome Traffic

The A12 running parallel to the Suffolk coast has a number of ghosts, including Black Toby who we mentioned earlier. A highwayman and his lady friend are seen at one point near Blythburgh White Hart. Animals seem terrified of certain places near the grounds of Blythburgh Priory.

A cyclist was once seen by a motorist coming towards him on the wrong side of the road. He swerved hard to avoid him, but the cyclist carried straight through the car. Turning behind him, the motorist swears that the cyclist turned his head towards him and gave a wide grin.

Whether this is also the ghost of postman William Ball is doubtful, since it is not certain that he would have had a bicycle. William died just after Christmas in 1899. He had been ill, but was determined to complete his round in freezing conditions that took him from Corton, Blundeston and Lound via Hopton. He was found frozen stiff and dead at the side of the road and his ghost has been frequently spotted, wearing a long coat and carrying two large sacks.